Seven Steps to wealth...

All the things they don't tell you about property investment

6th Edition

John L Fitzgerald

Seven Steps to Wealth

First published in Australia in 1998 by
Toogoolawa Children's Home Ltd. (ABN 73 053 100 351)
Reprinted 2011, 2013

©John L Fitzgerald 1998, 1999, 2000, 2003, 2006, 2010, 2011
ISBN 978-0-9757895-4-4

All rights reserved. No part of this publication may be reproduced, stored in a retrieval system, or transmitted, in any form or by any means, electronic, mechanical, photocopying or otherwise, without the prior permission of the publisher in writing.

Every effort has been made to trace the copyright holders of statistical information and diagrams reproduced in this book. The author is grateful to BIS Shrapnel, The Real Estate Institute of Australia, Residex, Business Review Weekly, ANZ Bank and the Australian Bureau of Statistics for permission to use selected data.

No responsibility can be accepted by the author or publisher of this book for any action taken by any person or organisation relating to any material contained herein. Property investment is a complex and constantly changing field, and all readers should seek independent and detailed advice as to the relevance of any part of this material to their own specific circumstances.

National Library of Australia Cataloguing-in-Publication data
Fitzgerald, John L., 1963-
Seven Steps to Wealth: all the things
they don't tell you about property investment.

6th ed.
Includes index.
ISBN 978-0-9757895-4-4 (pbk)

1. Real estate investment - Australia.
Other Authors/Contributors: Toogoolawa Foundation of Childrens' Homes
332.6320994

Text by John L Fitzgerald with Claire Louise Wright
Cover design by Kandream Digital Studios.
Designed and typeset by Evolution Creative Pty Ltd.
Illustrations by Dennis Holmes to concepts by Claire Louise Wright
Printed and bound in Australia by McPherson's Printing Group

Contents

	Page
INTRODUCTION	1
John L Fitzgerald	9
PART A: STARTING POINTS	
Start-up Quiz	21
1 Why build wealth?	25
2 Why residential real estate?	33
3 A structure for growth	51
PART B: SEVEN STEPS TO WEALTH	
4 Buy land for capital growth	65
5 Optimise your income	81
6 Maximise your tax benefits	101
7 Finance to build	111
8 Aim for affordability	127
9 Make time work for you	137
10 Be all you can be	155
PART C: ANY OTHER QUESTIONS?	
11 What about...?	169
Round-up Quiz	181
Quiz Answers	185
The Custodian WealthBuilders Group	191
Book Order Form	196
Donation Form	197
Product Order Form	200
INDEX	203

To Mary Fitzgerald.

We are all teachers.
Some teachers explain.
Some teachers complain.
Some teachers inspire.

Preface

This is not just a book about how to build wealth by investing in real estate. It's a book about how you can build wealth by investing in real estate.

There's a big difference. The words 'property investment' probably conjure up visions of serious guys in serious suits talking about things like 'negative gearing' and 'leverage' and 'equity positions'. And for most people, that's a major turn-off. Perhaps that's why property investment is one of the best kept secrets of the financial world.

I'm going to let you into a few well-kept secrets in this book – and I'm going to try and do it in easy-speak language that anyone can pick up and read. I figure, if Stephen Hawking can write a popular book based on Einstein's Theory of Relativity, then somebody ought to be able to do the same for real estate investment! I'd like to give you something you can relate to and, more importantly, use without constantly tripping over a load of jargon and statistics.

The books on wealth creation that are full of jargon and statistics (and there are a few of them about) are often written by academics who may have gathered a wealth of theoretical knowledge – but haven't actually, personally, created any wealth. I'd have to say, I'm pretty much the opposite.

However, Einstein himself said: 'Everything should be made as simple as possible, but not any simpler.' Good rule. So you will find numbers and charts and technical terms in this book, but they are there to clarify key concepts – not to prove that I can use statistics and big words! We'll also cover a fair bit of information, but this isn't one of those 'everything you never particularly wanted to know about economics' books. I'm simply going to tell you about the most effective way I know to build wealth.

At the end of this book, you will have a pretty clear idea of how to maximise your assets, reduce your tax bill, ask the right questions – and see through some of the so-called experts in the field. And, perhaps most importantly, you'll know that you can build wealth.

The principles set out in this book aren't new. I've been using them for myself, and for clients, for many years – and they work. They've given us financial freedom, security and a great lifestyle for ourselves and our families. And that's just one part of what building wealth is about. For me, it's also about the potential to make a difference in the world: an opportunity to be all I can be. I think of it as a journey to discover purpose.

Welcome to the adventure.

Foreword

6th edition

I am writing this foreword and updating this edition of *Seven Steps to Wealth* in the wake of the Global Financial Crisis (GFC). Some economists and commentators are saying this was the worst economic period in our life time and as bad as the Great Depression.

I don't think it was either of those, although it certainly was a test of every investment asset class. That in itself offers gems of wisdom.

It is amazing to see how many 'experts' there were saying the world was going to fall and prices were going to crash, especially at the end of 2008.

The most frequently asked question I'm asked by the media is: how has the GFC affected me and what am I doing differently? The answer is, it has not affected me and I am not doing anything differently.

This is how this book *Seven Steps to Wealth* has stood the test of time.

When I say every asset class has been tested, we have literally seen falls in the value of most, if not all asset classes. Shares were the first to crash with almost 47 per cent wiped off their value, for the second time in 21 years. Nothing seemed to be missed in the share market crash with all sectors bearing the brunt including 'blue chip' performers.

Real estate was also affected but different sectors of the market have been affected differently. The high-end housing market (houses over $2 million) dropped by 25 per cent and prices of high-rise units were hammered.

The middle to upper end ($700,000–2,000,000) fell 15 per cent and properties from $500,000–700,000 also dropped by approximately 10 per cent.

Similarly, commercial property is seeing the brunt of it now – most have fallen in value by 10–15 per cent in some areas and B and C class properties (the poorer cousins to A class property) may have fallen by 20–25 per cent.

As in 1993, banks are very nervous of commercial property, similarly of industrial property, farms, vacant land and businesses. Most of these commodities have seen values stripped about by the GFC.

So what stood the test of time? Pretty much one commodity: housing at the bottom end of the market. That is, houses under $500,000 within 30 kilometres of a CBD. In fact, after being flat for the second half of 2008, they actually increased in value in 2009 and continued through 2010.

You have picked up this book at a good time. The first edition was published in 1998 and in that edition, I referred to the recession of 1991–2 in creating this structure for Australians to build wealth.

The principles I used in the first edition are still very much alive and well today as the last recession and the GFC have taught us. That is, if you stick to one asset class as described in this book, then you pretty much can't go wrong.

The book is a bit more than just sticking to one asset class. It is a lot about solid principles for building wealth and there is no better than understanding compound growth. I want to mention compound growth up front, as it is important to your wealth building. I do it because so many people think you have to buy and sell, they get transfixed with what the market is doing – is it the right time to buy or sell, is the market going up or down. The truth is that has nothing to do with wealth building. Wealth building in real estate is about buying assets and using them to duplicate to other assets, enabling you to get compound growth.

It takes discipline – a lot of discipline. I love the saying, 'stick to one thing and do it well'. This is something else the GFC has taught us.

The companies, investors and businesses who survived the GFC are the ones who stuck to their core business, doing one thing and doing it really well. The ones who spread themselves too thin with too much debt did not survive.

I have been investing in real estate for 25 years. I have literally bought, sold and developed close to 10,000 properties and I still have a large portfolio.

You are going to get a lot of nuts and bolts advice on how to build a portfolio and hopefully you will get a taste of what it takes from your perspective.

It is about having the mindset to be successful, having that drive and passion. We will talk about this more through the book. This book asks you to adopt the success mindset of being positive, responsible and proactive.

The book asks you to be positive, to set clear and realistic financial goals to suit your aims in life – perhaps even your dreams. It will equip you to be responsible, to get to grips with how the wealth building structure works and how to make it work for you, in ways that are within your capabilities. It encourages you to be proactive, to get about there and do something with what you will learn.

It takes discipline and I am not promising you will get rich quick. I am saying you can build wealth, perhaps serious wealth, if that is what you want.

This book unravels some of the mysteries of property investment. I hope it will also give you a sense of responsibility, enough knowledge and confidence to take the first step on the road.

John Fitzgerald

September 2010

Introduction

A FOOL AND HIS MONEY ARE EASILY PARTED

There are really only two reasons why you would lose money in real estate:

1 greed
2 not doing your homework

Unfortunately, those two things catch out about 95% of 'punters'.

Greedy investors are usually locked into Get Rich Quick thinking – and they shoot themselves in the foot in all sorts of ways: making false economies, pricing themselves out of the market, and selling short of real growth. As an investor, unfortunately, you also need to avoid being manipulated by the greed of others – and there's a fair bit of it about in the real estate industry. That's why doing your homework is so important.

The real estate industry is huge: the residential sector alone turns over nearly $205 billion per year. That's a lot of property. And it's often bought and sold less on sound research and decision-making than on sentiment, impulse, gut feeling – and, of course, 'expert opinion'. (Multibillion-dollar industries seem to attract 'expert opinions' in about equal quantities.)

I forever have people walk into my office saying they've bought *the* property that is going to make them a lot of money, or that they represent a vendor or particular property that I've just *got* to acquire if I want to make money. Over the years, I have learned not to get too excited: probably 1 in 100 of these people has any idea at all what he or she is talking about.

It's a bit like McDonald's restaurants: everyone thinks they can set up a duplicate fast food chain, because McDonald's make it look like such a simple business. It isn't – and thousands have failed in the attempt.

I'm reminded of this every year, on my pilgrimage to the AFL Grand Final. Everybody has a strong opinion about the game, before, during and after it's played! Our opinions don't always coincide, and frankly, aren't always based on sober fact or objective analysis. That's our right to free speech! Sitting among the spectators, you could well believe that the person next to you would make a *far* better umpire than the umpire – and certainly a better coach than the guys in the box. The fact is, however, that umpires and coaches have paid their dues in the little league, or with other football clubs, and then graduated through the majors: they are appointed on their track record, and judged on their track record, game by game, as their career goes on.

> **There are literally thousands of people giving advice about what to buy or sell, and quite a lot of them simply haven't got a clue!**

The real estate industry has all the opinions – and not too many of the track records to support them. There are literally thousands of people giving advice about what to buy or sell, and quite a lot of them simply haven't got a clue! Others, of course, have their own good reasons for giving bad advice. And if you take that advice: sorry, but you are probably a fool – and guess what will happen to you and your money?

It sometimes seems like there's a 'veil of mystery' (or perhaps it's just confusion) over property investment. If you're going to make good decisions that will build you wealth, you need to look behind two veils.

1 Why are you buying a property?

2 Who is selling or advising you to buy it and why?

There are really only three reasons to buy a property:

- For your *own use:* that is, to live or work in.

- For *income:* that is, to supplement your income in the short-term, through charging rent, and taking advantage of legitimate tax deductions.

- For *capital growth*. That's what builds wealth. Add the dynamic of *compound growth* where you start with one property and use its capital growth as a springboard to acquiring more properties – and you have solid potential for *serious* wealth.

I travel all around Australia talking to people about building wealth in real estate. A lot of them have already acquired some sort of investment property, and when I ask, they are quick to say that, yes indeed, of course they're after capital growth. But a few more questions usually reveal that they never in fact considered the capital growth potential of the particular property that they acquired.

They 'knew' that property goes up in value, but didn't realise that that could mean anything from 20% per annum to 2%: in other words, the difference between positive and *negative* growth in real terms (in excess of inflation). They based their choice of property not on capital growth potential but on all sorts of other factors: they liked the idea of rental income (perhaps guaranteed by the vendor), or tax deductions; they 'liked' the property; it was recommended by someone they trusted; it promised low maintenance costs; it looked like a 'bargain'; the finance offered to them on the property made it amazingly hassle-free.

None of these things make for capital growth. If you're looking to build wealth: look past them!

Focus on capital growth. What is the property's history? What is its future?

Do you want to know what the single most important factor for capital growth is? *Land.* Land appreciates in value: buildings don't. However much you fall in love with a building, however low-maintenance it is, however much rent you can charge and however many deductions you can claim, the building will depreciate in value over time.

This is why so many investors get their fingers burnt with new units or townhouses. The land content of their investment may be only 10% of the purchase price, 90% of which is therefore a depreciating asset. This is the best-kept secret of the real estate industry because what developer is going to tell you

Do you want to know what the single most important factor for capital growth is? *Land.*

about it, when he can sell 20 units instead of a single house or duplex on the same block of land?

That's why you need to look behind the second veil: who are the people who are selling you the property and what are they getting out of it?

The real estate industry itself ought to do some housekeeping, but it comes down to the old Latin principle *'caveat emptor'*: buyer beware! Ask yourself a few awkward questions about the competence and track record of anyone selling or recommending a property and about their vested interests: what are they getting out of it?

You wouldn't believe, for example, how much heartache and loss of capital could be avoided by two simple questions:

1 Ask the agent to disclose the commission and marketing fees that the vendor is paying. Commission used to be regulated, but is now open slather in most states. It's a useful reminder: however co-operative they appear, agents work for the vendor (and themselves) – *not* for you, the investing buyer. Their interests – and those of their clients – are served by securing the highest possible price for a property: yours, naturally, are not.

2 Ask to see a copy of the bank's valuation of the property for security purposes. It is *not* always the same as the purchase price.

Sorry, but you cannot afford to be too trusting of the people you deal with. And that includes banks! Banks often lend on an investment property, knowing that the purchase price is way over their valuation of the property: they draw on your equity to make up the difference in the security – crippling your potential to build wealth. (Not that they disclose this to you! Some banks do have a policy to disclose their valuations, where there is a differential of more than 10%. This should be mandatory. It isn't. Some investors don't find out until a year or two later that they have an unexpected deficit in the calculation of their net worth.) I can assure you, banks would do things rather differently, if their right to recovery were limited to their valuation of the property!

Asking probing questions may be uncomfortable – but not nearly as uncomfortable as finding out that the equity you've built in your home over the past five to ten years has been wiped out because you didn't ask the questions.

> **Sorry, but you cannot afford to be too trusting of the people you deal with. And that includes banks!**

You need to listen carefully to the answers, too. Many of them may well come into the category of lies, damn lies and statistics! For example, one of the tricks of the property trade is for marketers to justify sale prices and their claims of growth by quoting newspaper clippings and comparable investment sales. Companies have been selling units in Sydney for years, by claiming that there has been a 20–50% growth in the value of similar properties – based on what other investors had paid six, twelve or eighteen months before. But this is not a true reflection of the market. Investors aren't the true consumers of property – and what's to say that those previous investors weren't likewise talked into paying an over-inflated price?

Previous investment sales are often a barometer – not of local market conditions, but of the effectiveness of a slick sales operation. My own home ground, the Gold Coast, has probably got the 'best' operators in this style: they sell literally thousands of properties each year to would-be investors, at 10–30% over the market value, using comparable investment sales to justify their prices.

And this is another reason to steer clear of units for investment: 60–100% of all units built are sold to investors not owner-occupiers. Which makes them a lousy barometer of market prices.

We'll discuss all these issues in detail, later in the book.

SO WHO AM I?

I'm asking you to look behind the veil of anyone who has an opinion about investment property. So what are my qualifications?

Academically, none. But in 1985, when I was 22-years-old, I started building a property portfolio that would have allowed me to retire very comfortably by the time I was 30. That in itself wouldn't make my advice better than the next guy's, but over the intervening period, I have bought myself literally thousands of properties, and now develop some 500–1000 residential properties per annum.

I have learned by experience how to create wealth consistently – and how to use it sensibly. And I have successfully helped others to do the same.

In any case, I'm not trying to turn you into yet another 'expert' on property investment and management. I'd like to get you focused on *capital growth* and *compound growth*, as a coach focuses a team on winning the game. I'd like to show you some of the pitfalls – so you don't have to fall foul of them the way I, and many others, did when we were starting out. And in the process, I may tell you a few things that don't usually get said in real estate circles.

Most importantly, I hope you'll realise that there are really *no* 'experts' when it comes to property investment. It's a bit like the weather: you can tell what it was like yesterday, and you might take an informed stab at forecasting what it'll be like tomorrow, based on current trends – but you know that conditions are changing from day-to-day and from place-to-place. The real 'expertise' is recognising that you're no expert – and staying on the ball.

> Sceptics make the best Wealth Builders.

I don't expect you to take my word for anything. I'd like to give you the confidence to go out and ask questions, demand evidence, investigate further. You won't be able to eliminate all your doubts or even all the risks: like any journey worth making, building wealth involves a few steps into unknown territory. But you can always test the ground. Sceptics make the best wealth-builders.

SO THAT'S WHAT THIS BOOK IS ALL ABOUT

In Chapter 1, I start explaining in detail how you can build wealth. By the time you reach Chapter 11, you'll have absorbed a lot of information (although I hope it won't seem too much like hard work at the time). You may even have changed your thinking.

It's a real confidence booster to be able to see that happening. So please, take a minute to fill out the short quiz on page *21*. You may already know some of the answers – but you may not. No worries, it's just like building wealth: you have to start somewhere! At the end of the book, you'll have the opportunity to do the quiz again. (And just like building wealth, you may be surprised how far you get!)

Who is
John L Fitzgerald?

This is another 'Introduction' – this time to me, and how I learned about building wealth. The point is, I'm pretty much an average person: if anything, a bit below average academically, and a bit above average in sport. I once bought a table tennis table ('flat packed for easy home assembly'). After half an hour wrestling with the instructions, I found a nearby 15-year-old who put the whole thing together, as advertised, in about 3 minutes.

If I can build wealth, you can. Seriously! And if that's all you really need to know, feel free to skip the next few pages and go straight on to Part A.

I was born in Melbourne in 1963 and spent my first eight years in the middle-class suburb of Moorabbin. My father was a menswear retailer and went into business on his own at the age of 30. By the time he was 37 he had built up three menswear shops in Collingwood, Belgrave and Stawell. He was a devout Catholic from an Irish Catholic family: five children, all in Catholic schools. My mother ran the home full-time, having left a career as a ballroom dancing instructor to marry Dad.

The school holidays of September 1972 changed my life – all our lives – suddenly and forever. My oldest brother David (then aged 12) went, as we often did, to visit Uncle Morris's farm near Shepparton. We heard later that he and our cousin Peter were lighting a fire when David, who was practising his notorious balancing act on a log, lost his balance and fell into the fire. Uncle Morris got him to the hospital, where he was found to have third degree burns from knee to ankle, and given skin grafts. I remember visiting David at the Shepparton hospital, the slick lino floors and the cold concrete walls.

He was there for six weeks. One Tuesday morning Dad drove out to visit him – and never returned. On his way home, the car was sandwiched between two semi-trailers and driven off the road: he was killed instantly.

At nine-years-old, I sensed that there was a purpose behind those rollercoaster days: I believed even then, that everything happens for a reason. That was the start of what I now see as a journey to discover my *own* purpose in the world – a journey which has since become linked to the creation and use of wealth. (If there's a 'bigger' purpose to your reading this book, I hope it will become clear as you read on.)

My mother had to take over the businesses, as well as run the family. She did a tremendous job, showing amazing business acumen for someone with no direct experience. To help her cope, we three boys were sent away to boarding school. I skipped Grade 6 in order to go to the same school as my brothers in 1974.

It was pretty clear from the first that I'd make my mark on the sports field, not in the classroom. I made the first 18 football team in Form 4 (Grade 10) despite being a year younger than my classmates, and I excelled in athletics and various other sports. All rather costly in terms of academic achievement... I left school in 1979, having just scraped enough of an aggregate to get my HSC. I was expected to go to university, or to repeat my HSC to improve my marks, but I had decided that the academic life wasn't for me. Boarding school makes you independent: I had hardly lived at home since I was 10-years-old, and the sum total of my worldly possessions fitted into a locker 1.8 metres high by 40cm wide. It was time to 'get in amongst it' and see what life was all about.

A friend and I had planned to hitchhike to Queensland (I wasn't old enough to have a car, being not quite 17).

In January 1980, the friend pulled out – and I packed a knapsack and headed off alone for the Gold Coast.

The Gold Coast was in the midst of a property boom, and I immediately knew I wanted to be a part of it. I applied for several real estate positions as a salesman and eventually, through contacts, got a start with Bert Cockerel, who had an office in Surfers Paradise. To call Bert a 'Jack of all trades' would be an understatement. I remember going round to visit a motel he owned on the highway in Surfers, called the Golden Sun Motel, now the site of a 30-storey high-rise tower called Zenith. Bert also owned the picture theatre at Palm Beach – and was an avid fisherman, who used to do the fishing report on the local radio station! A great guy.

> **The Gold Coast was in the midst of a property boom, and I immediately knew I wanted to be a part of it.**

I went round to see him about signing my application for a licence as a real estate salesman. I had to disclose to him that I wasn't yet 17, but Bert wasn't fazed by technicalities – and neither, it seemed, was whoever rubber stamped the application forms: despite being up-front about my date of birth, I was duly and officially licenced for real estate sales. (Does that make me the youngest ever? Perhaps it's better not to ask.)

Less than a year after I joined Bert, I was introduced to George Margolis, who had built a fortune in real estate during the 1960s – and lost it in the crash of 1974–75. Now, he was re-emerging from bankruptcy, and he had a good plan: with his knowledge and contacts, and my energy, we would make a tremendous partnership. So at 17 and 9 months old,

I became an associate partner of Cousins Real Estate. I still didn't know anything about real estate. Fortunately, I was a fast learner.

These were the heady days of the early '80s: looking back, 'incredible' is the word that comes to mind. At my age and with my experience (neither one particularly impressive), I could advertise for people willing to invest in a private property trust to develop units – and secure literally dozens of investors who were prepared to punt $50,000–100,000 on my ability to acquire a site, build a building and make a profit. Like I say: 'incredible'.

> **Fortunately, I was a fast learner.**

Of course, it wasn't just 'my ability': I had the building advice of a structural engineer who was part of the management team – and, of course, George Margolis.

BOOMS AND BUSTS – AND BAD DECISIONS

I remember all too well the high-rise buildings going up along Old Burleigh Road and the Surfers Paradise strip, where units would be settling in a building such as Aquarius. The developer would attend settlement, only to see the property transferred two or three times on the spot!

Greed, as ever, was the underlying factor: real estate agents were promising that if speculators bought, they could on-sell the unit immediately, because of the sky-high demand. It was not uncommon to see units, sold off the plan by the developer for $150,000–180,000, re-sell for $250,000, then $400,000, then $500,000 at settlement! (I call this the Bigger Fool Theory: if you invest in real estate on this basis, you have to be sure there's a bigger fool than you coming along behind, to give you a back door.)

> I call this the Bigger Fool Theory: if you invest in real estate on this basis, you have to be sure there's a bigger fool than you coming along behind...

On the heels of greed, as ever, came the crash. In 1982, you couldn't *give* high-rise units away for love or money! Literally tens of millions of dollars were wiped off the (over-inflated) prices paid by investors at the height of the feeding frenzy.

Developers also had their problems, notably Dainford Limited, which had built most of the high-rise on the Gold Coast and had just completed the Peninsula building, the tallest and one of the best located buildings in Surfers Paradise. A record number of people had acquired the units on the basis that they could on-sell them, found they couldn't – and defaulted at settlement.

The ups and downs of the early 1980s taught me a lesson very quickly: real estate is an ever-changing market – and while buildings are its prime 'product', it's the *land* that is the true, limited commodity. People repeatedly made the mistake of paying a premium above already over-inflated prices for a *building* which in itself was commonplace and easily replaceable.

Things haven't changed much: speculators are still madly snapping up inner-city units in Melbourne and Sydney, despite one in five currently having to take a *loss* on re-sale! (What percentage of Australians do you think buy units to live in, as owner-occupiers? Take a guess.)*

Just 6%!

BECOMING A WEALTH BUILDER

I acquired my first house and land package in Shailer Park, Brisbane, in 1985 for the tidy sum of $49,000. I borrowed approximately $47,000 on it – which sounded like a lot of money in those days. But that meant I could start out with just $2,000 of my own money – and today that property is worth over $400,000. That's where I started.

I had cottoned on to the fact that it was land that appreciated in value, not buildings, and that this created some rather encouraging mathematical effects: namely, if the house goes up by 10%, the land will go up by 20%. Armed with this information, and with a couple of houses under my belt, in 1987 I approached one of Australia's largest developers, Dainford Limited, and asked them to finance me into land estates. Dainford generally took 'long positions' in the market (that is, committed to projects which wouldn't provide income for 3–5 years), so my formula for acquiring land and immediately turning it into income was pretty attractive.

Our first project together was a 1,200 lot estate at Loganholme, south of Brisbane, which we acquired as an *englobo* parcel (before subdivision and infrastructure development) for approximately $2,500 per lot. Lots in that area at that stage were selling for around $25,000, and houses for around $60,000. As house values crept up to over $140,000, the raw land value rocketed to $90,000, forcing the *englobo* land up to approximately $40,000–50,000.

This sounds like a complete sweetheart deal, but for wealth building purposes, I wouldn't recommend it: land on its own generates no regular income (unlike a rentable property) and despite the potential for super profits, roughly 9 out of 10 land developers go broke in any 10-year period. I was one of the lucky ones.

In four years, Dainford and I developed and sold over 1,000 properties together. Yet, for all that activity, I realised I would have been a lot wealthier a lot sooner if I had constructed *homes* on 10% of the allotments that I developed and sold, and kept them as rental properties.

I have been in the business for over 25 years and I have bought, sold and developed close to 10,000 properties. I have probably made most of the mistakes that can be made – although I like to think I avoided a *few*, through seeing them coming. I gathered a pretty good idea of what makes a good investment, and how to make a good investment work better. I realised you don't have to be a property developer to build wealth in property. (In fact, rather the reverse: most of them go broke at one time or another, pushing for bigger and bigger projects.)

Since 1994, my company the JLF Corporation, has worked on a system – based on the structure outlined in this book – to facilitate wealth building programs for 'ordinary' Australians. (None of them ever turns out to be 'ordinary') We now hold public seminars on wealth building for anyone who is curious about the concept.

From the start, we set out to do things a little differently to other developers and marketing operations we know. We build relationships with our clients, beginning with their first property purchase. We've worked with those clients over the years, monitoring their capital growth and guiding them step-by-step to establishing a property portfolio.

And since 1998, our clients' properties have increased in value by more than $500 million.

It's been fascinating for me to see people come fresh to the idea of wealth building, and to see where they get to. Some of the people we work with are top sports people, who need to reduce their tax liabilities and shift their thinking from 'income' to 'wealth' for a future beyond sport. Others are those 'ordinary' Australians, who might never have thought beyond paying off their own home and earning a decent salary until they retire – but for whom the words 'financial freedom' (or is it 'millionaire'?) conjure up a whole new world.

I am really proud of the fact that some of our clients, who started with us many years ago, are now up to 5–6 properties. Many have 8–10 and some even have 10 or more. We have one investor with 19 properties and a family with over 30. In fact, Custodian WealthBuilders can boast creating 243 millionaires to date. I don't know of any other organisation with such positive results.

BECOMING A CUSTODIAN

And there's another dimension to it, for me. Whatever our clients' initial motivation to build wealth – and I guess we all start out 'self-centred' about this to some extent – I've watched person after person achieve more than wealth through the journey. Many have also found perspective and purpose: definitely, more-than-financial rewards.

I had my own major shift in thinking along the way. As you may have gathered, I knew from a pretty early age that I wanted to be wealthy: I set some ambitious goals for myself, and went after them aggressively. I got there – and then found that my perspective had changed.

There are very few wealthy people in the world. *Very* few. And I believe that it's pretty much up to those who control and enjoy the world's wealth to help those who don't! Once I had pulled myself into the former category, I felt the weight of that responsibility. I say 'weight', but I've actually found that the opportunity to use my wealth responsibly – to make a contribution to society – is one of the most joyful and enriching experiences of my life.

In 1990, I met a husband and wife psychologist team – Ron and Suwanti Farmer – and together we established the Toogoolawa Children's Home. Some of the wealth I have created, now funds unique educational opportunities for troubled youth, with Toogoolawa schools in three states (so far). I love the fact that my contribution can be the small difference that makes a big difference in these kids' lives – and so, I believe, in the future of Australia.

That's an important part of my story. I think it's an important part of wealth building, too, and when we help people to build wealth, we are not shy of urging them to think of themselves as *custodians* – as well as creators – of wealth that can make a difference in the world.

That's why, in 1998, we changed the name of our business, and now call ourselves – as we see ourselves – Custodian WealthBuilders.

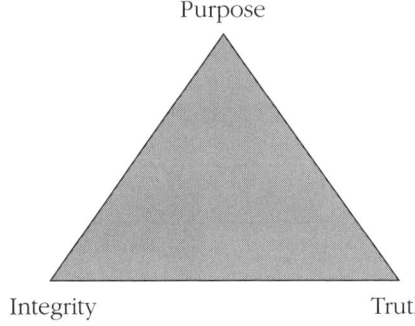

Purpose

Integrity   Truth

We express our corporate mission and philosophy quite simply and we encourage each wealth builder who joins us, to become a fellow Custodian.

Purpose: To create wealth

To serve humanity

Integrity: To accept responsibility

Truth: To keep questioning

Of course, none of this may be important to you right now. Feel free to put it all aside, just in a corner of your mind somewhere. Start building wealth for yourself and your family, to meet your future needs – or to set yourself a challenge. And as you build your wealth, and meet your goals, perhaps you'll remember this seed that I've sown. Perhaps you too will find something more.

On that note, let's move on to the business of building wealth!

Notes

PART A
Starting points

Start-up Quiz

The following are just a few questions to help us focus on wealth building, and to remind us where we are starting from. Don't worry if you don't know the answers yet: you will, by the time you attempt this as a Round-up Quiz at the end of the book!

1. In making a wealth building investment decision, what would be more important?

    ☐ How you felt about it
    ☑ How it stacked up logically

2. What has shown the higher investment return over the last 10 years?

    ☐ Shares
    ☑ Residential property

3. In buying a residential investment property for wealth building, what would be more important?

    ☐ Rental returns
    ☐ Taxation benefits
    ☑ Capital growth

4. If you invested in residential property, would you use the same criteria and decision-making process that you used to acquire your own home?

    ☐ Yes   ☐ No

5. Is it prudent for me to acquire property close to where I live?

    ☐ Yes   ☑ No

6. What would be more important in acquiring an investment property for *wealth building*?

    ☐ Managing your cash flow

    ☑ Buying the right property

7. What type of property would show the highest capital growth?

    ☐ Unit/townhouse

    ☐ House

    ☑ Land

8. If you had $50,000 deposit to invest in property, would you be better off buying:

    ☐ One property for $100,000?

    ☐ One property for $300,000?

    ☑ Two properties for $150,000 each?

9. The median house price in Brisbane rose from $30,500 in 1977 to $440,000 in 2009.

    ☐ True   ☐ False

10. If you bought a house in 1967 in Melbourne, Sydney or Brisbane, by how much has its value increased in 2005?

    ☐ Doubled in value   ☐ 10 times (1,000%)

    ☐ 5 times (500%)   ☐ 20 times (2,000%)

11. Which institution(s) effectively control the affordability of housing in Australia?

    ☐ Real Estate Institute ☐ Banks

    ☐ Property developers ☐ Valuers

12. Is the number of renters of property in Australia:

    ☐ Increasing? ☐ Decreasing?

13. The Pay As You Go (PAYG) Income Tax (including Medicare Levy) on a salary of $60,000 is approximately $12,150.

    ☐ True ☐ False

14. Can I use my PAYG Tax to build wealth?

    ☐ Yes ☐ No

15. In choosing a location that is going to give capital growth, which factor is most important?

    ☐ Proximity to transport

    ☐ Proximity to schools

    ☐ Percentage of investor-owners

    ☐ Established capital benchmark

16. You are seeking a bank loan for an investment property. Rank the following criteria in order of priority.

    ☐ Interest rate of loan

    ☐ Interest-only loan

    ☐ Full disclosure of bank valuation of investment property

    ☐ Non-collateralisation of other property

17. What is the 'established capital benchmark' of an area?
    - [ ] The median price of property in the area
    - [ ] The highest price of property in the area
    - [ ] The lowest price of property in the area

18. What was the average land size of an urban house in the capital cities in 1970?
    - [ ] 450 m²
    - [ ] 600 m²
    - [ ] 750 m²
    - [ ] 1,000 m²

19. What was the average land size of an urban house in the capital cities in 2009?
    - [ ] 450 m²
    - [ ] 600 m²
    - [ ] 750 m²
    - [ ] 1,000 m²

20. What was the percentage growth in the median price of a typical high-rise unit between 1999–2009?
    - [ ] 4%
    - [ ] 8%
    - [ ] 6%
    - [ ] 10%

Sorry, but I'm not going to give you the answers at this point! That's what the book is for. Forget about this quiz altogether, for the time being.

At the end of the book, you'll get to tackle the same questions again. With answers provided if, by that time, you need them...

Chapter 1: Why build wealth?

DO YOU WANT TO BE WEALTHY?

Silly question, right? *Everybody* wants to be wealthy. Imagine the security and the freedom. Imagine retiring with enough money to do all the things you've wanted to do, for as many years as you've got – and not having to rely on the government for a cent!

It seems extraordinary, but when we surveyed 2,200 people in the south-west Brisbane area, 78% of them said they 'never thought about building wealth'.

Let's look at it another way.

How much do you reckon you'd need – per year – to live comfortably in retirement? I'm not asking you to do budgets and calculations and adjustments for inflation (although at some stage, if you're talking to an investment advisor, it would be a good idea). I'm just talking ball-park figures: what kind of a sum per year would you want to retire on, in today's dollars?

> **Nearly all of us want to be wealthy – and nearly all of us retire below the poverty line! What's going on?**

Most of the people I talk to would say something over $50,000 per annum (even though the median wage in 2009 was closer to $70,000 per annum).

Your own estimate: $_____.

That estimate may be perfectly realistic for your own financial circumstances: you'd have to do a few calculations to find out.

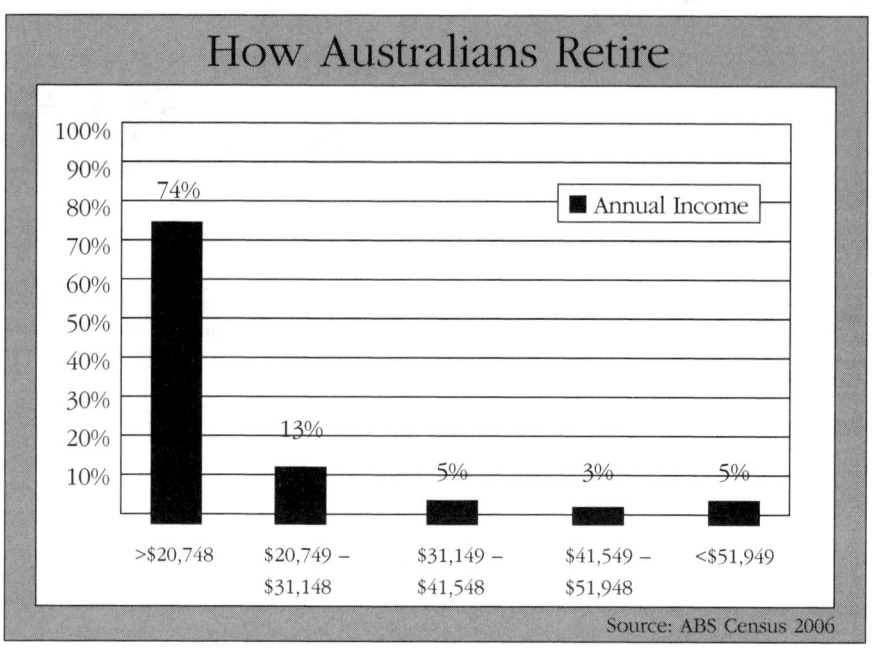

But the following chart shows what Australians actually *do* retire on.

Nearly all of us want to be wealthy – and nearly all of us retire below the poverty line! What's going on?

To retire on $50,000 per annum, you actually need around $1 million in assets *and* to own your own home.

And that's in today's dollars. In 20 years' time, with inflation at 4%, the equivalent sum would be $100,000 per year, requiring $2 million in assets.

How many of us have a plan in place to build up those kinds of assets by the time we retire? Apparently, only 5 in 100 of us! If you are one of those, please accept my congratulations and best wishes, and feel free to stop reading (although there may be a few things in this book that will surprise even you). If you are *not* one of those, it's *your* responsibility to change this for yourself! (Think about it. On whom would you want to be financially dependent when you retire? The government? Your kids? Read on...)

WHY AREN'T MORE AUSTRALIANS WEALTHY?

There are a number of answers to this question. (I haven't included 'waiting to win the Lottery' – although, with $75 billion 'invested' in gambling in Australia each year, you'd think we were pretty serious about this as a retirement plan!)

We don't have enough money to build wealth

Wrong. The structure I'll show you in this book allows you – even encourages you – to start small. You only need a combined annual gross income of $60,000, and a small amount of cash or equity in your own home or other property, to get started. Wealth is accessible to most Australians. Mostly, it's about using the resources you have, and restructuring your cash flow. And all that takes is (a) knowing how and (b) choosing to give it a go.

Our parents never taught us to build wealth

Most people my age were taught that we would grow up, get a trade or a university degree and then a job: we'd save up enough money for a deposit on a house, and we'd use our work income to pay off the loan on that house over 25 years – and *then* maybe we could consider another investment. Sound familiar? Well, that's exactly what most Australians do.

I call this 'income thinking'. We need to replace it with 'capital thinking'.

There's always a safety net

I think this is part of the same thing. Our grandparents seemed to live fairly happily on the pension in the post-war years, and in the '50s and '60s, Australia enjoyed a relatively high standard of living compared to other nations. Of course, that was when there were about 18 taxpayers for every pensioner. Today, there are less than 6 taxpayers per pensioner, and if demographic trends continue, within 20 years there will be less than one taxpayer per pensioner. Meanwhile, because we're living longer, the average Australian will have to fund at least 20 years of retirement.

It won't be long before the government simply won't be able to afford the age pension – even at its current meagre levels. So we might like to think about making our own arrangements.

We don't like debt

This is something else our parents taught us. There are some sound values behind it – self-reliance, pay your own way – and it's true that escalating debt is a concern. But we need to distinguish between debt on consumer items that depreciate in value (like a car, a dining suite,

Today there are less than six taxpayers per pensioner. In 20 years...

28 Seven Steps to Wealth

or a stereo system) and borrowing on an asset that *appreciates in value* and *generates income* (like property). The latter kind of debt (a) supports the borrower's ability to make the necessary repayments, and (b) offers a profit on sale of the asset.

On the other hand, you could buy a new BMW Cabriolet (say) for $100,000, and by the time you drive it out of the showroom, it's only worth $85,000: if you borrowed $100,000 on it, you're already facing a deficit of $15,000, which you have to pay off. Each year, more of the same: you could end up making payments of $12,000 for four years – and still face a balloon payment of about $70,000 (which may, or may not, equal the capital value of the car by that time). Now, *that's* debt.

Ironically, people routinely run up thousands of dollars in 'small' debts on consumer items – but baulk at taking on a mortgage.

Let's get debt into perspective. You can't build wealth without acquiring substantial assets for capital growth – and you can't, realistically, do that without borrowing the money to invest: that is, *'gearing'*.

It's an income world

What does 'being wealthy' mean to you? Some people might say: a big salary, with a lifestyle to match. But that's not how wealth works. Income by itself doesn't make you wealthy. You spend some. You save some (maybe), and inflation gradually wears its value away. Capital, on the other hand, is material wealth which can be used to produce more wealth, by investment. Capital grows, income flows (mostly, through your fingers.)

Unfortunately, most people don't get past income: they don't get their money growing and working for them. The system is there – but only capital-focused people use it to build wealth.

You can't *save* your way to wealth.

Wealth building is strictly for whizz-kids

Some investment advisors would like you to think so. But the good news is that property investment need not be the sole preserve of financial experts. By the end of this book, you'll know enough about 'leverage' and 'negative gearing' to get by. You'll have a simple investment structure and clear principles to work with. And if the whole business seems like too much of a hassle – remember, you don't have to do it all yourself! You can get advice and help with everything from working out an initial budget to managing a whole portfolio of investment properties.

Custodian WealthBuilders is just one example of an organisation that offers a whole range of services in the property investment field, or you could get advice from other sources. Look behind the veil. Try and find someone who has actually done what they are advising you to do! This goes for accountants, financial advisers and real estate agents: there are some good ones who have built wealth – and that's the first credential I'd look for.

Wealth building is strictly for sharks

It's easy to get that impression – and not everybody relates to the idea that 'Greed is Good' the way we seemed to when Michael Douglas said it in the movie *Wall Street* in the early '80s.

I think we need to challenge the way we think about what wealth is for. Sure, it's about quality lifestyle, providing for family, a financially secure retirement, control over your future and all that good stuff. But it is also about *responsibility*.

As I outlined in my personal story, the Custodian philosophy is that those few of us who are fortunate and informed enough to build wealth can – and must – choose to use it responsibly. Wealth puts us in a position to help those in trouble and need – and to shape the kind of fair and hopeful society we would want our children to inherit. It's also our responsibility to educate the next generation to manage and preserve capital, for our nation's financial and social wellbeing. Custodian WealthBuilders believe that this is what true investment in the future means – and we find that it yields the most valuable and satisfying returns.

> Sharing in the custodianship of our society's future is one way of being all you can be

We encourage all fellow wealth builders to adopt this philosophy. This book is about what's possible – in all sorts of ways. Sharing in the custodianship of our society's future is one way of being all you can be.

WHAT'S THE SOLUTION?

At the risk of sounding like a sportswear advertisement, it's quite simple:

Just think differently!

JUST THINK DIFFERENTLY: CAPITAL, NOT INCOME.

When we talk about 'wealth building', we are talking about:

- establishing a *structure,* or system, to manage your *cash flow*
- to acquire *assets* (in this case, residential real estate)
- for *capital growth:* that is, to increase the value of your investment over time.

Your investment may, of course, also offer you income and tax advantages. But it's the capital growth that counts. It's the capital growth – combined with compound growth – that makes millionaires.

And as it happens, most millionaires achieve capital growth by investing in real estate.

This book will take you step-by-step through how it all works, and what you have to do.

Chapter 2:
Why residential real estate?

If you just look at results, you'd have to say that property seems to make good investment sense.

For example, it is, consistently, a major source of wealth for the wealthiest Australians. (And 90% of millionaires worldwide.)

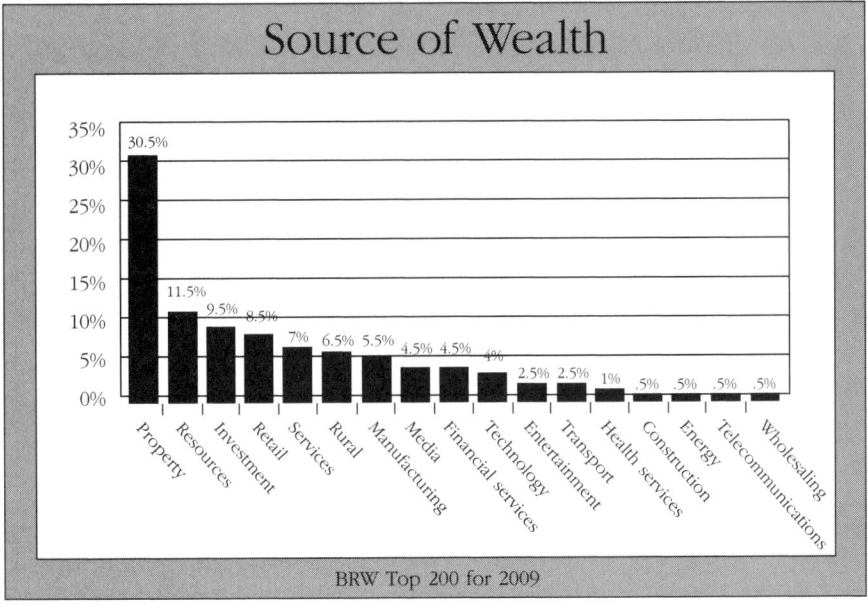

Residential real estate, in particular, scores pretty high on just about any quality you'd look for in an investment – remembering that your purpose is capital growth.

☑ SECURITY

Residential real estate offers the security of 'bricks and mortar' compared to the fluctuating values of shares and commodities – and even compared to the manageability of commercial and industrial properties, over the medium- to long-term. Even allowing for the ups and downs in real estate values we all hear about, the underlying trend shows remarkably steady growth.

You can see this trend quite clearly in the following table and also in the graph on the next page depicting house prices over the last 30–40 years.

House Price Growth

	Sydney	Melbourne	Brisbane	Adelaide	Perth
	$	$	$	$	$
1967	15,000	13,000	9,700	10,000	10,200
1977	44,000	38,000	30,500	32,800	38,500
1987	120,600	89,400	62,300	77,700	61,200
1997	235,000	175,500	140,500	114,000	135,300
2005	518,000	375,000	320,000	277,000	325,000
2009	544,000	540,500	535,000	539,000	480,000

Source: REIA March 2009.

In fact, the growth pattern has stayed pretty constant throughout the last century.

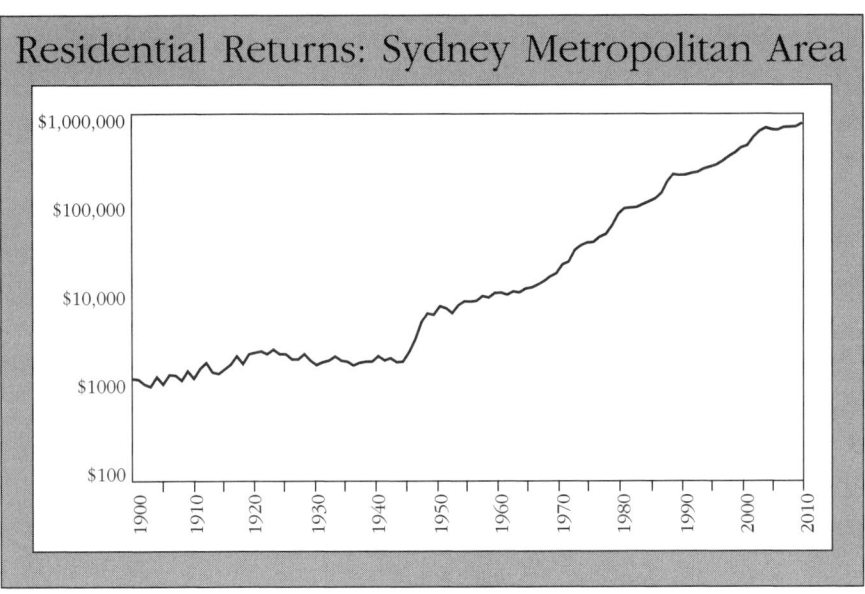

Residential Returns: Sydney Metropolitan Area

Roughly speaking, this means that residential property has historically *doubled in value every 8–10 years.* And don't forget that as the population continues to grow, the demand for housing must continue to increase.

☑ PERFORMANCE

The following graph by the ANZ Bank (2009) shows residential property as the best investment asset class over the past 25 years.

And these are just averages. The better your real estate investment strategy is – where you buy, what you buy, how much land content and how you finance – the better the returns can be.

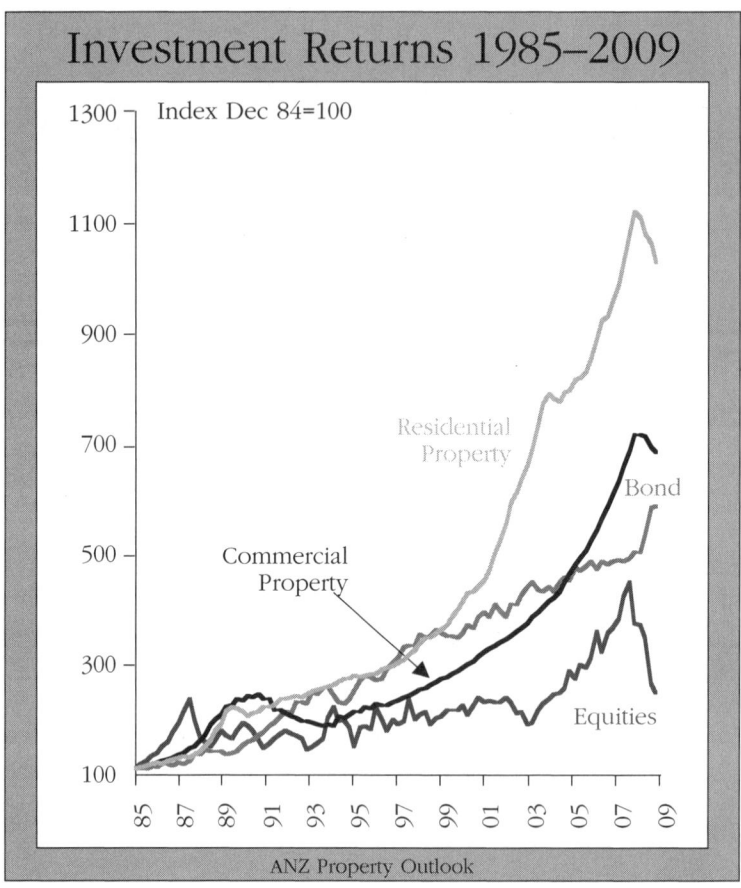

Some of the statistics actually downplay the performance of property. Take median house prices, for example. Over the last 20–25 years, the median house price in most of the capital cities has increased by between 8–11% per annum. But look at that 'median house' in the 1980s: it's on a standard quarter acre allotment, or 1,000m². Look at the 'median house' today: what with urban sprawl, the standard lot size has decreased to about 450m²! Remember: it's the land value we're mostly interested in. If you look at the actual value of that quarter acre block in the capital city, it has well outperformed the supposed 'median house price' and presented huge wealth building opportunities – particularly with the advent of dual occupancy or sub-division.

✓ LEVERAGE

Because of its security and performance, residential real estate also represents 'security' (in the legal/financial sense) or collateral for loans. Most banks regard residential real estate as prime security, against which some will lend up to 90–95% of the property's value.

Definition
Gearing is borrowing money for investment.

'Leverage' in mechanics is a way of turning a small amount of force, at a strategic point, into a much greater force. (Think of a car jack.) Financial leverage works the same way: you can use a small amount of money to acquire an asset of much higher value, on which you reap larger returns and growth. (This is a key factor in the performance of property, as compared to shares, as a long term investment. We'll look at it in more detail, below.)

Definition
Leverage is gearing your investment so that the proportion of capital you invest is low in relation to borrowings: say, 20 : 80 or 10 : 90.

Equity is your 'net worth': the value of assets that is actually yours, or accessible to you: in other words, the value of your assets *minus* the debt you owe on them.

If the value of an investment property goes up, and the mortgage on it stays constant, your equity – or '*net worth*' – increases.

Basically, the high degree of leverage on residential property allows you to build wealth by using just a little of your own money – and quite a lot of other people's!

This is great news, because it means you don't have to be wealthy to build wealth! Residential real estate is actually one of the most *affordable* investments around.

> **You don't have to be wealthy to build wealth!**

The banks' confidence in residential property allows you to use your increased equity as security in a fairly liberal way, to piggy-back one purchase on another and build up a portfolio of properties – as we'll show you in Chapter 3 – so that you benefit from compound growth.

WHAT ABOUT SHARES?

A lot of people will try to tell you that shares are a better investment than property. It's true that some shares show a higher income return. They are easily tradable, and shares in the major companies have the advantage of high liquidity: they're practically cash. In fact, prior to the crash of 2007–08 shares even measured up to property based on annual returns. Obviously, that will change with the Global Financial Crisis (GFC) and the All Ordinaries Index falling by around 47 per cent. Shares are rebounding but they have a long way to go – and property may equally well be at the peak of its cycle. So let's acknowledge that both show good capital growth. I'd still argue that property is the better investment. Why?

The difference is the *leverage*. You can buy property on a 10% deposit, because it represents a bankable security. When it comes to shares, however, most banks will only lend 50–60% of the purchase value.

Here's an example: Bill and Ted both have $40,000 in cash. Bill puts his down as a deposit on a property, while Ted uses his to buy shares.

Let's assume that in the first year, the value of Bill's property increases by 9.8% – and Ted's shares go up by 12.6% Which was the better investment?

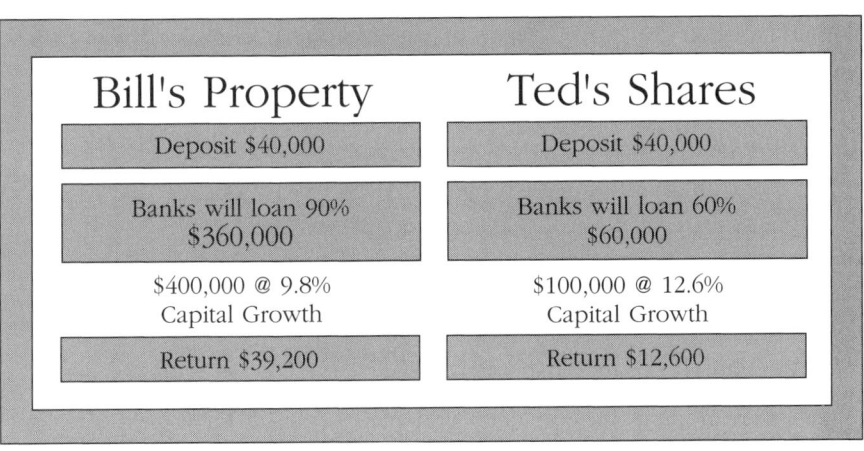

Even if the shares have twice the 'growth' factor, the property offers more than twice the growth in true capital worth (equity) – simply because of its leveraging ability.

Bill gets over three times better a return in property.

Bill's *equity* has gone up from $40,000 to $79,200 ($439,200 – $360,000). That's a return of just under 100%.

Ted's equity has gone up from $40,000 to $52,600 ($112,600 – $60,000): a 32% return.

So even if the shares have twice the 'growth' factor, the property offers more than twice the growth in true capital worth (equity) – simply because of its leveraging ability.

Chapter 2 - *Why residential real estate?* | 39

Property's reliability makes a difference, too. When banks lend on shares, they usually reserve the right to a *margin call* should the shares drop in value. (A margin call is where you are required to provide a cash top-up to maintain the agreed loan-to-security-value ratio. So if you borrowed 50% of the value of shares, and their price dropped, you would have to pay off part of the loan so that the outstanding amount still represented only 50% of the value of the shares.) This can be scary, because some banks can give you just two or three days to rectify: if you have a falling share price, you could be topping up on a daily basis!

Banks *don't,* however, require a margin call on 3–5 year loans on property particularly at the lower end price bracket. So there's no risk of them selling you up because of a temporary hiccup or glitch in the market!

WHAT ABOUT COMMERCIAL PROPERTY?

Commercial property includes land and premises used for retail, offices, industry, entertainment and hospitality; anything from the corner store to the Westfield centre. While residential property values are expected to maintain their rising trend, the future for commercial and industrial property is much less certain – and that's generally reflected in the amount banks are willing to lend. Moreover, while the growing demand for rental property allows you to be a relatively passive investor in residential housing, you can't take the same kind of back seat with commercial property.

When you buy a commercial property, you're buying land plus buildings plus goodwill. If the property is tenanted, its purchase price will generally be based on the rate of capital return it offers which may be a far cry from the building's replacement value. Let me give you an example. A friend of mine used to develop Big Rooster (now Red Rooster) outlets. He purchased the land for around $80,000 and built the premises for around $100,000, with car parking and landscaping and so on. He then leased it to Big Rooster for a whopping $40–45,000 per annum, and sold on – showing a 10% return. This is good development business.

The point is that an investor buying a Red Rooster outlet is paying a premium of $200,000 for goodwill – in effect, for Red Rooster's continued success. But if Red Rooster left those premises at the end of the lease, you would be left with an empty shell, with a replacement value half of what you paid for it, and limited ability to attract new tenants, since it was purpose-built for a particular fast food chain.

There are some real horror stories since the GFC. For example, people borrowed to invest in companies that no longer exist such as Westpoint, Timbercorp, Great Southern and Storm Financial. Tens of thousands of investors were burnt.

Horror stories about margin calls are not just related to the companies that went broke. They also relate to the big 'Blue Chip' companies as their shares also lost significant value. This made the banks call on their margins and investors needed to come up with the cash within 2–3 days. In many circumstances, the banks sold the shares and then pursued those investors for the balance of their outstanding debt. This resulted in some people having to sell other assets or even their own homes. From my perspective, margin loans are a very high-risk way of investing in shares and making money, especially if you do not have the cash to meet the margin difference.

I remember an investor telling me he had found the perfect way to build wealth. He had bought large tracts of land and leased them for a 10 per cent return to the emerging timber companies Timbercorp and Great Southern. He said he could buy these properties for $800,000 and with the timber companies renting them at 10 per cent, he could see no better way to make money. I told him the Red Rooster story: how they were bought out and closed many of their shops so it was unwise to put all his eggs in one basket – especially in an industry as fickle as growing trees supported by tax savings.

Early in 2009, both Timbercorp and Great Southern went broke. They ceased making payments and left investors with large areas of land with small trees growing on them. The land has almost negative value because it does not provide income in its current state and the cost of clearing the land to provide income would cost $100,000s. Future use of the land would also be subject to council approval and potentially rezoning.

Businesses come and go – and not just geographically. You have to think about the retail areas around you. The last 20–30 years have seen the mushrooming of regional shopping centres, which have squeezed out many strip shops and neighbourhood shopping centres. They come complete with entertainment and refreshment facilities so you can stay all day and pick up a few more impulse buys. With the advent of 24 hour shopping, it seems only a matter of time before these shopping centres and petrol station/convenience stores completely take over.

I am not saying all shops are bad, what I am saying is leave it to the specialists and big companies. Some of the biggest and best in the world do it very well and even so, they too experienced tough times during the GFC.

It is a similar story with office buildings. Office tenants will come and go and the office buildings will often age quickly and require you to spend money on capital works and lease fit out incentives as well as taking risks on tenants, which during a downturn could be high. The better buildings will

> **Businesses come and go – and not just geographically.**

rent well but these are $10 million investments – not what you would call a starting point for average Australians.

Banks look at commercial property differently compared to housing. I do have a sizable commercial portfolio but it is something I have dedicated managers working on almost full time. When the banks reviewed my debt levels during the GFC, they did not blink on my housing debt but they did require me to get all of my commercial properties revalued and then they wanted me to lower my loan value ratios to below 70 per cent of the new valuations.

I am not saying commercial property is a bad investment, but it is a specialised one for a small investor. If you are keen, you could invest in property trusts with a range of commercial properties enabling you to spread the risks of tenant downturns. However, while commercial property offers a reasonable income base, it does not have the best potential for capital growth or for duplicating your success to build a portfolio.

MEANWHILE, THE FUTURE FOR HOUSING...

Fortunately, we all have to live somewhere. And the wonders of modern technology still haven't provided any alternatives to living in some form of 'housing'. (Indeed 'houses' are still the norm, outside medium- to high-density urban areas). We also know we have long-term housing growth because Australia currently has the highest population growth on record. This growth is occurring through migration since we have such an aging population. In fact, we are not only short of houses now, but we will need a lot more homes over the next 20–30 years to cope with that growth needed to replace our retiring baby boomers in the workforce.

AREN'T WE ALREADY INVESTING IN RESIDENTIAL REAL ESTATE?

One of the things I like about residential real estate is that it is a known quantity for a lot of people. They may not be entirely comfortable with the language of finance and banking, leverage and gearing, but they have *some* experience of the sector, especially if they own their own home. This can be pretty reassuring, if you're sticking your toe in the shark infested waters of investment for the first time: at least you *know* that you know how to choose and buy a home.

Sorry, but actually this makes for rotten investment decisions!

It's a bit like taking up snow skiing.

If you haven't snow skied, it's a great sport – and if it's accessible to you, I recommend that you give it a try. I learned some of the basic principles when I was a kid, but only took it up again about 10 years ago, having water-skied for many years. And now, on my annual visit to the snowfields in Victoria or New South Wales, I'm constantly reminded of two things:

1. Snow skiing and water skiing may look vaguely similar, but if you try to snow ski the same way you water ski – you end up on your face (or worse). The apparent familiarity makes you feel pleasantly confident, but it can also blind you to the fact that the principles and techniques involved are quite different.

> At least you *know* you know how to choose and buy a home...

Logic and emotion can give you two conflicting messages

2. Logic and emotion can give you two conflicting messages – and if you're doing something that 'feels' risky, it's the feelings that shout loudest! When you're on top of a mountain, thinking about heading down, logic and science and the ski instructor and all those good things are telling you that to stay in complete control, you need to lean down the mountain, with all your weight on your downhill leg. Meanwhile, your emotions are telling you to keep your bum as close to the snow as humanly possible! It's easy to say 'go with the logic', and I'm the first to admit that, for a novice, hurtling down a mountain at 30–40 kph doesn't feel 'in control' at all: and, yes, the temptation to lean cautiously back into the slope is fairly powerful. But that's the reason you see me, and a fair few others, losing control on the slopes and ending up with our bums *on* the snow. We let emotion, not logic or science, make our decisions for us.

And that's exactly how too many people invest in real estate. They take the (largely emotional) experience they have in choosing their home, and try to apply it to choosing an investment property. Logic and science go out the window – and so does capital growth.

So what *are* the right criteria to use?

CHOOSING A HOME

When we choose somewhere to live, we naturally go with our emotions, gut instincts and lifestyle choices, and quite rightly: this is going to be our home. We walk into a place with our partner, having looked at several properties – perhaps not even knowing what exactly we're looking for – and suddenly we're in love. It's the place of our dreams (or looks like it could be, with a little work).

I had exactly the same experience buying the property where I used to live. My fiancée and I had been looking for months, and because of our lifestyle we particularly wanted acreage land near water. On a rainy Saturday afternoon, I drove up the driveway of perhaps the twentieth property I'd looked at. I got out of the car and knew instantly: this was the one. I made an offer on the place before I was halfway through the front door – and without even consulting my fiancée. Talk about risky decision-making. Fortunately, she had exactly the same response to the place when we went back together the next morning – and of course, we did eventually get around to going through cupboards, flicking switches and checking carpets.

Later, I pulled down that house and built another one, and I am the first to admit I completely overcapitalised on the place as an investment. Even so, it was a great way to buy and make a home! If you're happy in your own place – be happy. You need to 'feel at home' where you live: it makes a huge difference to your work and other areas of your life.

But it's not the way to invest in residential real estate for capital growth.

CHOOSING AN INVESTMENT PROPERTY... NOT!

I always seem to get people coming up to me, bragging that they've started 'wealth building', and all excited because they've just purchased an investment property to take advantage of negative gearing, et cetera, et cetera. They sound like they've won Lotto – and they want to tell me all about it.

They spoke to their accountant and bank manager, got the tick, and went off in search of a property. Their first port of call was the local real estate agent, because after all, they'd purchased their home through him, and they'd got chummy over the years. And would you *believe* it? The Perfect Property had just come on the market – Just Around the Corner from their home! Old Mrs Reid's house was for sale: she was moving into a retirement village – signed a contract to purchase a unit. It was such a big house, and she couldn't look after it any more. And what a bargain! ('She's asking $500,000, but I'm sure if you made a cash offer you could get it for $475000...')

Our couple can't believe their luck. They've driven past Old Mrs Reid's house a thousand times, always admired it, and now they not only get the chance to buy it – they can get it for a full $25,000 discount on asking price! Within 30 days, they've got themselves an investment property...

Why did they choose this particular property? 'It's ideal: *we can drive by it every day on our way home from work!'*

> Does that sound like a dumb reason? It does, if your purpose is to build wealth.

Does that sound like a dumb reason? It does, if your purpose is to build wealth. (In fact, our couple has broken just about every rule in this book.)

And do people really *do* that? It sure looks like it. Of the Australians who own residential investment properties:

26% INVEST WITHIN THEIR OWN POSTCODE!

CHOOSING A PROPERTY FOR CAPITAL GROWTH

Here's where the logic and science come in. There are three questions we need to ask ourselves, if we want to invest in residential real estate for capital growth:

1. What **structure** will best utilise my cash resources to allow me to build up a property portfolio in the shortest period of time?

Chapter 2 - Why residential real estate? | 47

2. What **sort of property** will give me the highest capital growth?

3. What **location** will give me the highest capital growth?

Unfortunately, most Australians who invest in property don't ask themselves even *one* of those questions – let alone all three – which is why 97% of them don't maximise their capital growth or their tax benefits. And why only 1% of them build enough wealth to retire on an income (in today's terms) of more than $50,000 per annum.

Just one more statistic: less than 15% of all property investors buy more than one property. But *one* property won't make you wealthy. You need to focus on building a *portfolio* of five or six properties over 10 years. The good news is, this catapults you to the very top – that magic 1% – of successful investors in financial security and freedom.

So it's time to ask – and answer – the three big questions. We'll start with structure, in Chapter 3.

Notes

Chapter 3:
A structure for growth

In order to build wealth, you need to:
- establish a structure
- to acquire assets
- for capital growth
- and then duplicate the process to develop a portfolio.

Why do you need a 'structure'? You need a structure because there are different elements involved in making your investment work. You've got land and buildings, equity and loans, tax and tax benefits, rental income and outlays, and time. The mix and balance of all these elements needs to be just right in order to *accelerate portfolio development* and *maximise capital growth* – and it needs to be do-able time and time again. If you can work out what the 'best fit' is, and set it out as a simple formula, you can achieve predictable results – without having to juggle all the balls in the air all the time!

And you can *duplicate* the strategy without having to re-think it every time! Remember: one property won't make you wealthy. You need to use the equity growth in that one property to acquire a second, third, fourth – a portfolio of properties *all* providing (compound) growth. *That's* when it gets exciting!

Building wealth using property is a bit like building muscle using weights.

There are a different elements to building muscle.

The weights are only the *vehicle* you use to build the muscle. (Some people seem to think just owning weights is good for you – but it's using them, and how you use them, that counts.)

Technique is important. You need to use a weight that is within your capacity, and to lift it correctly, in order to stretch a specific muscle. Then you can gradually build up to heavier weights.

Diet is all-important to 'fuel' the exercise. You need the basic energy of carbohydrates, a reduced fat intake, and an increased intake of protein, for specific muscle growth.

Finally, *rest* is essential. The muscle actually only grows when resting after being stretched.

A weekly or fortnightly exercise routine incorporating all these factors would provide an efficient, effective structure to follow.

Start small, think big!

OK, SO BACK TO WEALTH BUILDING!

An effective structure for wealth building will incorporate the same kind of elements.

- A 'vehicle' for building wealth: in this case, residential real estate. The *land* is the vehicle for capital growth, and the *building*, for generating rental income.
- A 'technique' which will maximise the effectiveness of the vehicle for your purpose of capital growth. You need to select a suitable vehicle: the *right property*, in the *right location*. And you need to start – and stay – within your *financial capacity*: at the bottom end of general affordability, where most people can afford a first property. As you see growth, you can begin to build up a portfolio: more properties, not more expensive ones.
- 'Fuel' for your investment. With a basic level of available equity and income, you can secure *finance*. With the right property and the right lender, you can borrow 90% of the purchase price. You put in just 10% of the capital – and access 100% of the capital growth. That's the beauty of leverage.

> You're setting things up so that there's a lot to gain – and not a lot to lose.

In order to make this work, without draining your personal resources, you need *income* from the property, to service the debt. If you optimise the rental income and maximise the tax benefits available, you can effectively offset *all* your outlays: not just the loan interest, but also maintenance, rates, fees and so on. As long as your costs are covered, you won't be putting any strain on your cash flow – and you shouldn't be able to get into too much trouble! In other words, you're setting things up so that there's a lot to gain – and not a lot to lose.

Chapter 3 - A structure for growth | 53

- Meanwhile, you need to let your investment 'rest' in order for it to grow. Over time, the value of the property (in particular, the land component) increases, and – since your debt stays the same – your *equity* also increases. Once you have a 10–15% increase in value, you can use the extra equity to 'fuel' the purchase of a second property – and so on, and so on, using exactly the same formula, and with no further claims on your income or other assets!

At the end of a 10 year period, you can have built up a portfolio of, say, 6 residential properties this way. If they've shown sufficient capital growth (and remember, house prices have doubled every 8–10 years over a century) you need only sell one or two of them to reduce your borrowings on the whole portfolio. Which leaves you with strong equity in the remaining properties, plus the on-going rental income from them.

The overall structure can thus be illustrated as follows.

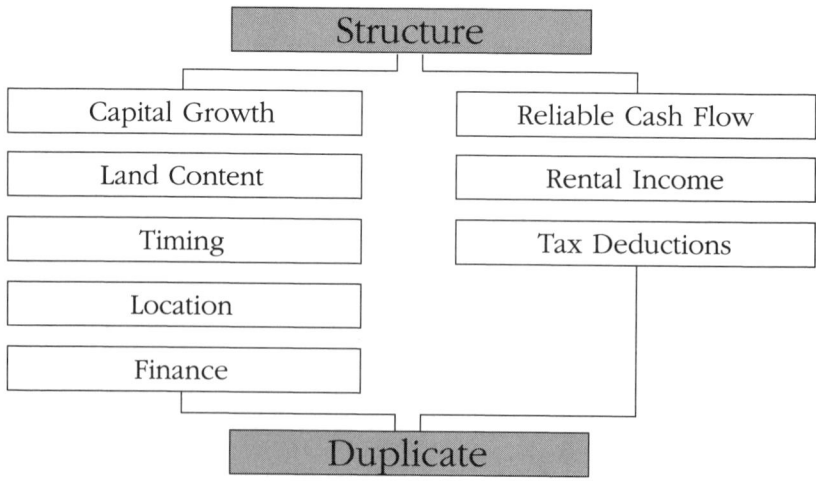

If all this seems too good to be true, I can tell you that it is possible: I'll be showing you how.

Case example: McDonald's restaurants

McDonald's restaurants is one of my favourite examples of a system based on real estate.

When Ray Crock established the McDonald's franchise system in 1954-5, the menus consisted of only nine items, and the restaurants prided themselves on being able to sell and serve a 15-cent hamburger inside 60 seconds. By the end of the '50s, there were more than 80 restaurants across America, each franchise sold for around US$900: franchisees also paid Ray Crock a percentage of their investment as a franchise fee to cover administration. Unfortunately, huge business growth can't be sustained by limited capital – and therefore limited capital growth – and in the late '50s, McDonald's nearly collapsed under its own weight.

What saved McDonald's to grow into one of the outstanding businesses of the 20th century? Structured investment in real estate. The company acquired all the restaurant properties and then leased them to the franchisees – retaining management of some restaurants themselves. In the following decades, this strong real estate base financed the building of thousands of restaurants all over the world. McDonald's is today worth billions of dollars because of a fundamental decision to restructure their cash flow, allowing them to acquire property, and to secure a steady demand for tenancy (through the success of the franchise), thus generating rental income. They started out with little or no equity.

That's pretty much how our structure works: supplying property to willing tenants (within an affordable price range) to finance the building of a real estate portfolio for sustained capital growth.

HOW IT ALL WORKS: AN OVERVIEW

1: Gearing

You borrow 90% of the value of an investment property, giving you 10% equity. All it takes is 10% growth in the property's value – and you have 100% return on the capital you invested, per annum!

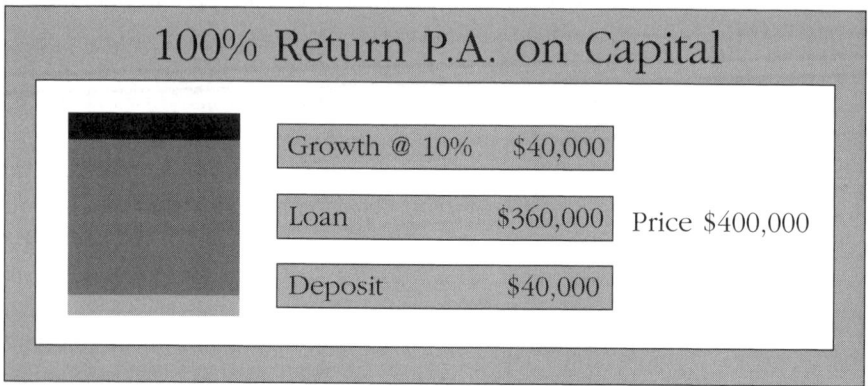

100% Return P.A. on Capital

| Growth @ 10% | $40,000 |
| Loan | $360,000 | Price $400,000
| Deposit | $40,000 |

Your 10% could represent a cash deposit, or you could use the equity in your own home, which may be more tax effective. (I'll deal with this in Chapter 7.)

2: Cash flow management

But what about the loan interest and all the other costs of doing this? Surely they eat away at your 100% return? No: that's where the structure comes in. It's all about *cash flow management*: the basis of all successful businesses.

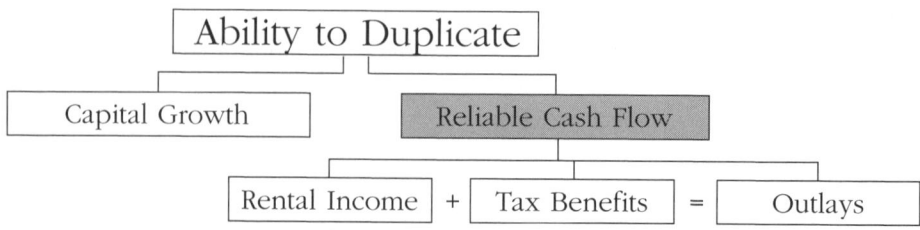

Ability to Duplicate → Capital Growth, Reliable Cash Flow → Rental Income + Tax Benefits = Outlays

3: Equity growth

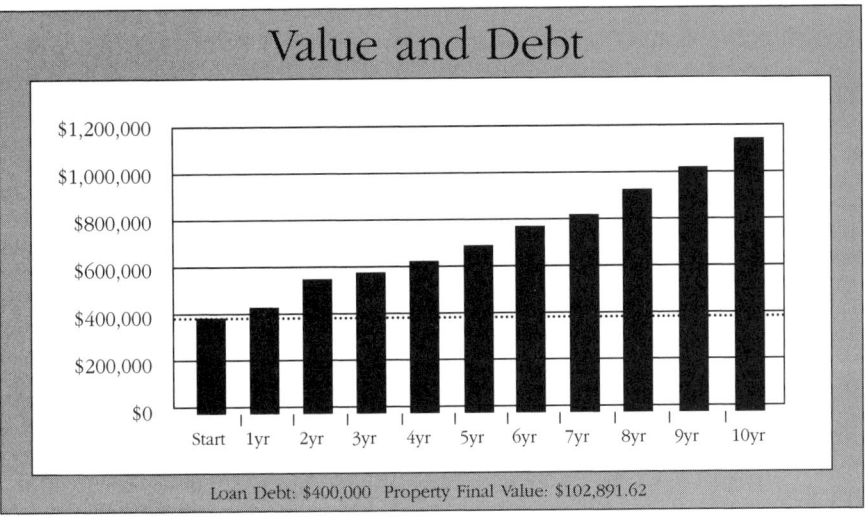

You need 10–15% equity growth to give you the 10% equity you need to duplicate your strategy with your next property. And repeat. And repeat again.

If there's a warning bell ringing at the back of your mind about the *debt* you'll have chalked up by this time, don't worry: I promise to put that into perspective later on.

THE STARTING POINT

You can begin to build wealth now if you have:
- about $60,000 annual (combined gross) income
- and $50,000 in available equity (in your home or other property) or cash deposit (although there are ways of getting round this too.)

Don't forget, you needn't actually pay out any of your income. It's just an indicator of your ability to repay a loan: one of two criteria – equity being the other – on which banks and other institutions lend money for property investment. (In fact, you could actually *increase* your net income, thanks to tax savings, as we'll see in Chapter 6.)

THE BEAUTY OF COMPOUND GROWTH

If I took just one cent and doubled it each day, how long would it take to turn it into a million dollars? The answer is: just 27 days. Sounds amazing, doesn't it? That's the power of compound growth: growth on growth (on growth...).

The following graph shows how you can access that power, from the minimum starting point cited above.

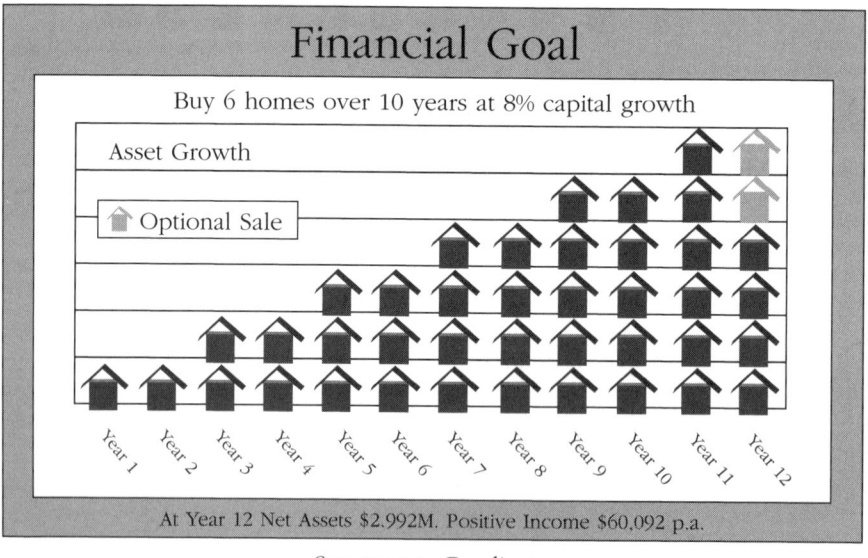

Structure to Duplicate

HOW MUCH CAN YOU ACHIEVE?

Here's a slightly more aggressive use of the same structure.

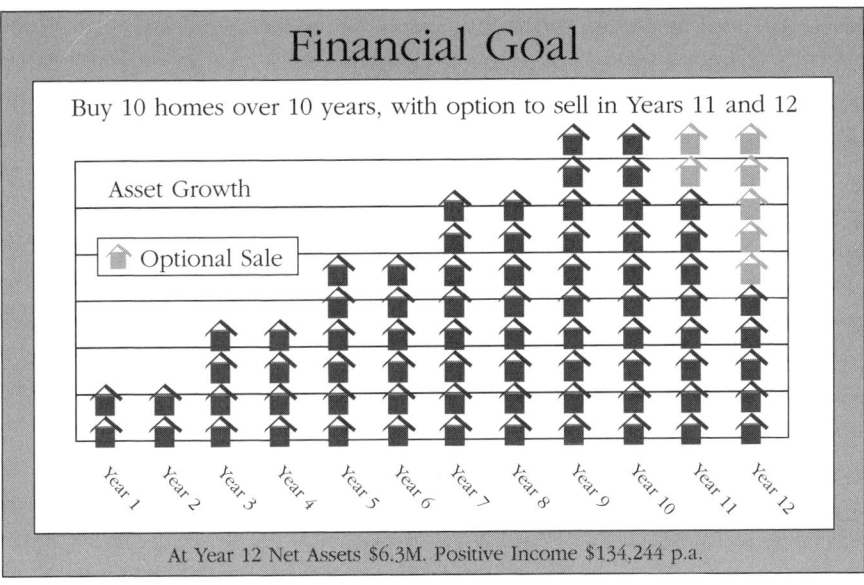

I can't tell you what your goals or commitment should be or what your potential is. It has to be up to you.

My best advice is: allow yourself to start small – and to think big.

After more than 12 years of coaching investors, many clients have 6, 8, 10 homes and more. Some clients have as many as 15–20 homes. They started small and built momentum. As the capital value of their properties and their income grew, they were able to duplicate to achieve compound growth. Many of them are now millionaires and multimillionaires by using exactly this system.

WHAT DOES IT TAKE TO MAKE THE STRUCTURE WORK?

We've already mentioned the key elements – but let's get specific. There are seven basic steps to building wealth:

1. Buy land for capital growth.
2. Optimise your income.
3. Maximise your tax benefits.
4. Finance to build.
5. Aim for affordability.
6. Make time work for you.
7. Be all you can be.

In Part B, I'll deal with each step in turn.

Notes

Notes

PART B
Seven steps to wealth

Chapter 4
Buy land for capital growth

[Step 1.]

If you take away only one thing from this book, make this the one.

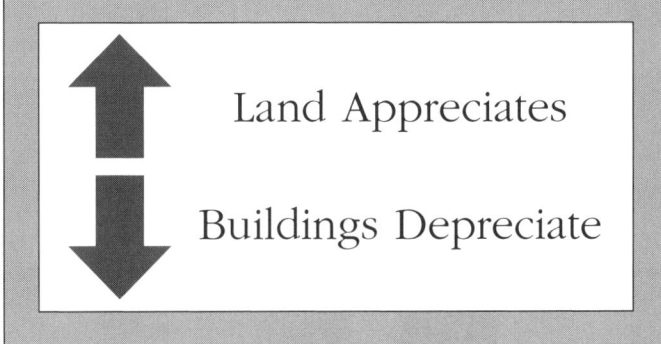

Land Appreciates

Buildings Depreciate

It's all to do with supply and demand. Land is a commodity which is obviously limited in supply, and for which demand is continually growing, as population increases. 'Bricks and mortar' are pegged to inflation and labour costs, so their price does go up – but they are not, as yet, in limited supply: buildings are pulled down (sometimes, before they fall down) and are easily replaced.

If you extract the land value from the growing value of house prices over a 30–40 year period, you can see that the land actually increases in value by nearly *twice* as much as the house value. As a compound effect, land in any 10 year period shows capital growth of around 15–20%, depending on location. The building component depreciates, effectively reducing the property's investment value – although inflation can camouflage the lack of capital growth. (During the '70s, just about everything went up in value by 10–15% per annum, but the lower inflation rates of the '90s have unmasked the real extent of growth.)

As an example, here's a graph showing the growth in house and land values in Brisbane over the last 30 years. Quite astounding from a growth perspective wouldn't you say!

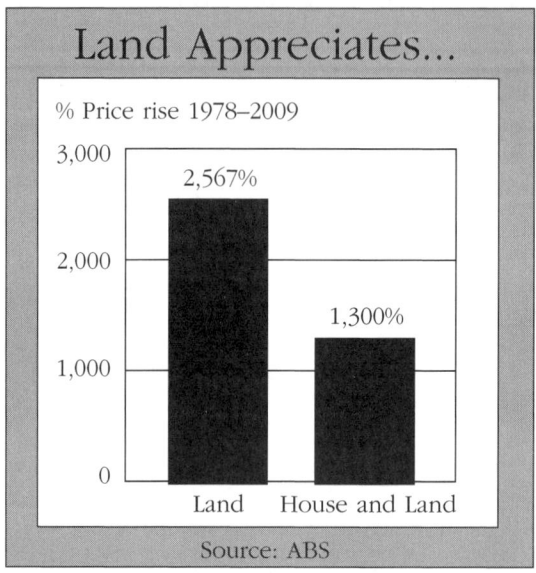

Unfortunately, if we are starting out with limited capital, we can't just buy land: we need a vehicle for generating income to service our debt. That vehicle is the *rental property*. But knowing that the land is the appreciating component, we need to acquire rental properties *with the highest possible proportion of land content*.

Take a look at this:

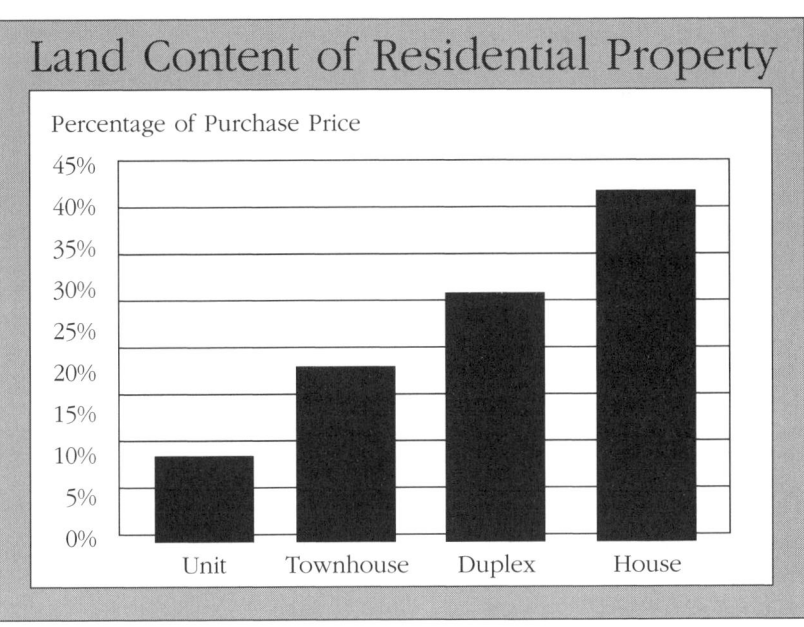

In order to achieve real capital growth to allow you to build a portfolio over a 5–10 year period, you need to have *at least 30% land content*. (I usually look for 40% +).

Duplexes and houses fall into the category of effective wealth building assets, with 30%+ land content. Townhouses within 7km of a CBD *can* also sneak into this bracket. (Check before you jump in.)

The 'good old' suburban home has the highest land content, and invariably gives the best capital growth.

BUT THEN – WHAT ABOUT UNITS?

I'll say it again: in order to achieve real capital growth over a 5–10 year period, you need to have at least 30% land content. With most units and townhouses, you are lucky to find 10–15% land content within the purchase price.

Say you bought a residential unit as an investment over a 10–20 year period – as some 34% of investors do. The proportion of land value to building value is perhaps 10 : 90. Land appreciates, buildings depreciate – and you end up with limited capital growth (other than inflation) for the first five to ten years. This is *not* the way to start building a property portfolio.

I have to tell you that the statistics don't support me on this one! Median house price growth in Sydney, Melbourne and Brisbane has averaged 8.26–9.44% per annum over the last 20 years. And units have averaged 7.58–9.13%. Not that bad, surely?

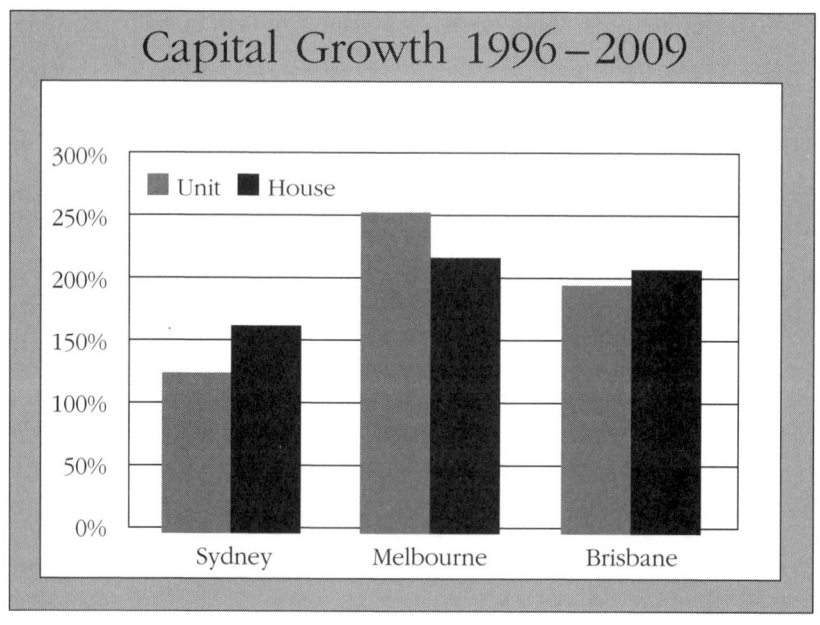

Most units have very little land content

You need to look *behind* the numbers. The majority of units sold are *new* units so the median figure is *predominately made up of new prices*. If you tracked the percentage growth of an actual unit bought 20 years ago (as you would in the case of a house) you would find that it really only averaged 4–6% growth. The statistics are effectively comparing oranges with lemons – and making lemons look good.

The fact is, a one-bedroom unit is just about the worst investment you can make (particularly if it's less than 50m²). It scores low on capital growth (no land) *and* on leveraging ability: you can borrow between 90–100% on a standard investment house in a capital city, but you'll be limited to

Chapter 4 - *Buy land for capital growth* | 69

60–70% on a unit (particularly high-rise). In fact, a mortgage insurer requires a unit to have a minimum internal floor area of 50m² (40m² in some city metropolitan locations) for it to even be considered as security on a loan.

Forget the hype: four in five buyers are, over the long term, taking a loss on CBD units in Sydney and Melbourne, bought off the plan. Why? Because only one in five of them buy to live in: the rest are speculators, who don't tend to look level-headedly at the real facts of supply and demand.

Yes, you will always find people who advise you to buy units. Don't buy land, they say: you'll incur land tax; tenants don't like mowing lawns; it's easier to find tenants for units than for houses.

Look behind the veil. The fact is that developers can make a healthy profit from selling units with nominal land value: is it any wonder they forget to mention that it's the *land* that appreciates?

Capital City	Median House Price	Land Tax
Sydney	$529,926	$2,690
Melbourne	$444,595	$644
Brisbane	$414,909	Nil
Adelaide	$404,921	$1,105
Perth	$473,292	$398

State	Threshold
New South Wales	$376,000
Victoria	$250,000
Queensland	$600,000
South Australia	$110,000
Western Australia	$300,000

Developers make a healthy profit from selling a number of units with nominal land value: is it any wonder they forget to mention that it's the land that appreciates?

As for land tax, it's there – but it's not nearly as bad as they make out. The unimproved land value has to exceed a set threshold (calculated differently from state to state) in each state. In Queensland the threshold is $600,000. And you only pay tax on the land value in excess of that amount.

A cautionary tale

Dainford Limited developed thousands of high-rise units in their time, but they rarely held on to any, because they found that they tended to lose their value.

This came home to me during the early '80s, when units had dropped in value, and one of my associates went on a buying rampage. He clinically offered just 60–65% of the price that a unit had sold for, less than three years previously, in nearly a dozen buildings across the Gold Coast. He held the units for ten years and sold them again, averaging a 13.5% per annum growth rate on his purchase price. He had the financial capacity to buy multiples of units and to make cash offers to desperate vendors.

In hindsight, he could have achieved the same kind of growth – without having to deal with desperate vendors, and without taking a huge cash outflow on the chin – simply by buying *houses at market value*. (He would have done even better, if he had bought *new* homes, and claimed the depreciation as a tax-deductible item, as discussed in Chapter 6.)

The real cautionary moral of the story, however, is the depreciating value of the units. My associate was able to buy them, second hand, at a capital *discount* of 30–40%. It is almost like buying that new BMW Cabriolet and driving it out of the showroom knowing that, as you cross over the grate, its value is probably dropping by 20–30%.

Case example

One of my favourite 'land appreciates, buildings depreciate' stories comes out of Queensland's Gold Coast. A guy bought the property (pictured next page) in 1974 for $87,000 – and sold it in 1995 for $1.075 million. The house was a pull-down job, though rentable: the $1.075 million represented land value only! (Today, remarkably, the house is worth over $8 million. So selling in 1995 – even at a great price – may not have been the best option. Sometimes, the best option is: don't sell! Keep the growth working for you.)

DOES THE LOCATION MATTER?

Location is *vital* for capital growth.

I recently ran a wealth building workshop for high-income individuals in Melbourne. At the start of the workshop, half of them affirmed that they were already investing to build wealth. I asked what their properties were, and where. Answer: they were units, in and around inner residential Melbourne. I asked what the land content of those units was. Answer: a sea of confused faces.

These people – competent, clued up people – had acquired units in the area where they lived, purely on the basis that they would be easy to

You *have* to do some homework – or find someone to do it for you.

maintain and manage: a classic case of the 'I can drive by it on my way home from work' factor.

You *have* to do some homework – or find someone to do it for you.

Case example

A good friend of mine is the manager of a top hotel in Sydney: a very astute guy. In 1994, he invested in the Canberra residential unit market, and acquired two townhouses there. When I asked him why, he said he did it for the tax benefits and to make some money. Wrong. His investment has actually showed him a loss to the point where the $60,000 capital he originally invested has all but been wiped out, and in 1997–98, there was no market for his units, due in part to the government's decentralisation policy: there was a population exodus from Canberra, which kept him in the abyss for another 3–5 years. That's the wrong way to start your portfolio. Do your homework!

SO WHERE SHOULD YOU BUY FOR CAPITAL GROWTH?

The key factor is *demand*. And demand for residential property is underpinned by:
- population
- employment and
- lifestyle

There are macro and micro factors involved here.

The *macro* point is that the greatest growth of population and employment on an on-going basis is going to be condensed in the capital cities. The diagram on the following page shows projected population growth over the next 50 years: Brisbane and Perth obviously stand out. Employment opportunities are also more abundant in the capital cities, because they are home to established industries – and industrial diversity (unlike regional areas, as we'll see a bit later). The *micro* point is that people – individuals and families – decide where they want to live. When I'm building a portfolio, I base it on the following demographic factors.

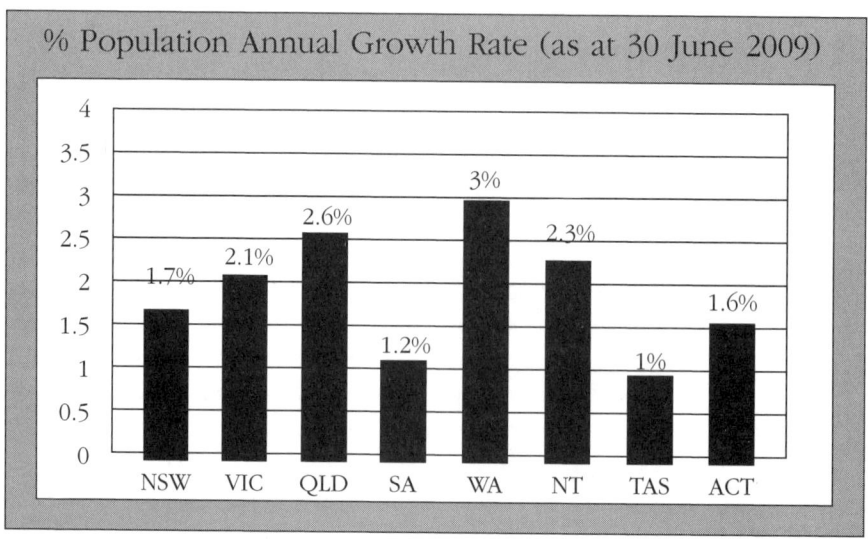

% Population Annual Growth Rate (as at 30 June 2009)

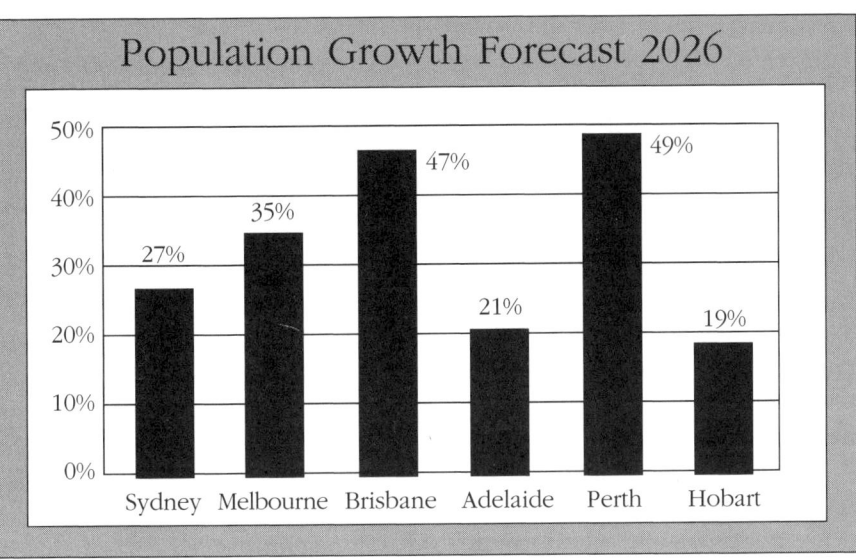

- *Population per household*

In 2001, there was an average of 2.6 people per household. The Australian Bureau of Statistics (ABS) has projected household size to continue to decline to 2.2–2.3 people per household by 2026 which is mainly due to the aging population. While this is a significant decline from 3.3 people 35 years ago, it is an urban myth that the average household size is 1–1.5 people.

- *Lifestyle choices*

  The Urban Land Institute identifies six main reasons why families with children live where they live.

  1. Schools
  2. Family security
  3. Transport
  4. Shops
  5. Employment
  6. Recreation

Every single one of my investment properties is *within 5 kilometres* of (private) schools, shops and transport.

Every single one is in what I classify as a secure family oriented area: an area with a population as close as possible to 3 people per household, where at least 7 out of 10 households are owner-occupiers – not investors. (You can get those statistics from the Australian Bureau of Statistics.)

How does this contribute to capital growth? If a suburb has 3+ persons per household and 70% owner-occupation, there's going to be a strong demand from owner-occupiers – and, often, their friends and family. With private schools nearby, they will tend to stay in the area for 10–20 years, depending on the age of their children. Owner-occupiers also tend to recapitalise their homes, upgrade and maintain their grounds better than investors, injecting further demand – and capital – into the area.

And that's where another factor enters the picture.

THE BENCHMARK FACTOR

The potential value of a property in any given area reflects the *best* or highest value of property in that area: this is called the *'established capital benchmark'*.

When I buy an investment property, I'm looking to buy in an area where I can pay substantially less than (maybe half or one third of) the capital benchmark: the price my neighbours have paid to get into the area. This is what some people call 'the worst house in the best street': it represents great potential for immediate capital growth. I'd forsake some of my other location criteria to find it.

Picture two houses.

Neighbour's House   My House

The house on the left cost over $300,000 to build on a $120,000 block of land: the house on completion was worth about $450,000–500,000. (It sold in 2005 for $760,000.)

The house on the right is one of my investment properties. I paid $100,000 for my block of land and $107,000 for the house.

I invested $207,000 to be located next door to someone who had invested over $400,000. Within 18 months, my house was revalued at over $320,000.

That's great capital growth – thanks to the reflected value of the area as defined by the established capital benchmark: the highest property price in the area. (Even better, I didn't put a cent of my own money into the house. In the first year, it cost me less than $2 per week – and thereafter, it was cash flow positive! That's the beauty of our structure, as we'll see.)

If you want assured capital growth, buy in an area where there is a capital benchmark set by owner-occupiers, who have been prepared to pay two or three times the price you will have to pay. That means a bit more homework on the Internet, or perhaps driving around – but that's what effective real estate investment is all about.

WHAT ABOUT REGIONAL AREAS?

As we noted earlier, the demand for property is likely to be most consistent in capital cities.

Many investors buy into regional markets because they seem more affordable, or they show better rental returns. But my experience has been that whenever there's a hiccup, it's those areas that are hit hardest. When they suffer economically, unemployment figures can rise quickly – and with them, rental vacancy rates. That's one reason why banks aren't as bullish about offering 90–100% loans (high 'loan-value ratios') in those markets: another brake on your compound growth.

I have had experience in the regional markets of Gladstone, Coffs Harbour, Cairns and even as close to a capital city as the Gold Coast. I have also witnessed, first hand, the problems experienced in Canberra and Newcastle when a dominant local employer decides to relocate.

In a capital city, you have major industries feeding off each other, and a major population base which can attract new investment and further population growth.

Because we are talking about building up a portfolio, we could be in a position – in 10–20 years' time – where we have accumulated 10–20 properties in a particular area. If a principal employer relocates or suffers financial strain (as with the government moving jobs out of Canberra, or BHP moving out of Newcastle), the area can free-fall into a downward spiral for anything up to ten years. Geelong, in Victoria, is another regional market that suffered badly during 1990–91, through the financial collapse of a major building society and the shut-down of manufacturing businesses: years later, the area hasn't yet bounced back, although the general property market in Melbourne has shown a solid recovery.

I live on the Gold Coast. I love the Gold Coast. I said in earlier editions of the book, however, that I classed it as a regional market: not an area to build a significant portfolio. Well, I've had to revise my thinking, as the area has pushed through the 500,000 population barrier – and *still* has population growth forecasts that outperform all the mature cities.

There have been some significant updates to population growth forecasts since the 2006 census compiled by the ABS, which is relevant to building a property portfolio. The big picture is that Australia's population is aging – nearly 25 per cent of our population are baby boomers (born 1945–60) who will retire in 2010–30.

Government and business have recognised the need for skilled migration to replace retiring baby boomers and as a result, migration is growing at record numbers. In 2008, Australia had its highest ever population growth on record of nearly 390,000, with skilled migrants making up 230,000 of that number. The ABS forecasts that by 2026, if only 180,000 skilled migrants enter the country each year in next 16 years, the population will grow by 6.9 million people to around 28 million people! Even after the recent debate of reducing our skilled migrant intake due to rising unemployment, the Government only cut it to 210,000.

Here is the other key point: of the 6.9 million population increase, nearly five million will go to the four main capital cities of Brisbane, Melbourne, Sydney and Perth. Adelaide is very much the poor cousin with only about 20 per cent of what the other cities average. Each of the four capital cities will increase in population by over one million people except for Perth, which is tipped to increase by approximately 800,000 – significant for the size of the city.

It reinforces what I wrote in 1997 – stick to the main capital cities.

The GFC has crystallised the shortage of housing accommodation in Australia, which was reaching crisis levels in 2005–07. Rents have been rising in the main capital cities by 10–15% per annum, due to the shortage of supply. The GFC has meant this will become more acute through 2010–12.

Personally as an investor along with thousands of our clients, we have received 10% rental growth for the past few years, in a climate that also reduced interest rates. While interest rates appear to have stabilised, it is a great cash flow position to be in.

SUMMARY

LAND APPRECIATES, BUILDINGS DEPRECIATE

☑ Invest in a house/duplex with at least 30% land content.

PROPERTY APPRECIATES WITH DEMAND

☑ Invest where population and jobs are growing.
☑ Stay within 45 minutes' drive of a capital city.
☑ Locate close to schools, family security, transport, shops, employment and recreation.
☑ Buy low in an area with a high established capital benchmark

And how do Australians currently invest in real estate?

34% BUY UNITS

26% BUY WITHIN THEIR OWN POSTCODE

No wonder most of us retire on welfare.

The beauty of getting this decision right, however, is that by buying in a growth area, you not only maximise the capital growth on your property: you also have a high tenant population from which to generate rental income! We'll talk about rent and renting, in Chapter 5.

Chapter 5 [Step 2] Optimise your income

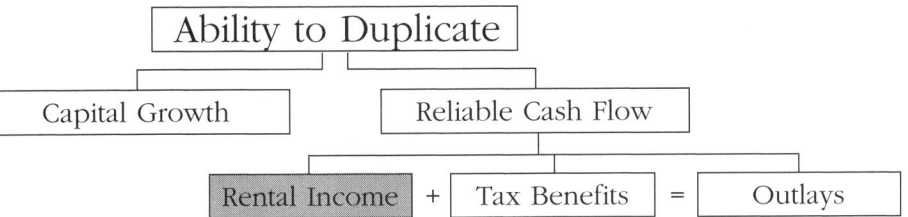

The beauty of gearing and leveraging your investment is that you can begin to build wealth with minimal capital, borrowing the balance of the acquisition costs of your first investment property. The downside is that you have to service that debt. And then there are other outlays, like maintenance and rates. The property doesn't pay for itself. Or does it? Residential property, as we've seen, has the potential to generate *income* to offset your cash outlays, while its capital value increases over time. Income is the fuel for capital growth. For 'income', read 'RENT'.

WHO RENTS AND WHY?

Ninety-five per cent of Australians have rented residential property at some time. More to the point, 30% of Australians *currently* rent residential property – and the number seems to be increasing.

There are increasing numbers of older people, empty nesters, DINKS (double income, no kids) and single parent families in our population, and these categories tend to push up the demand for rental property. Another factor is that property price increases tend to outstrip inflation (which is great for capital growth) and therefore also outstrip rises in wages and salaries: the rental market grows, as property prices gradually rise beyond the reach of more and more people.

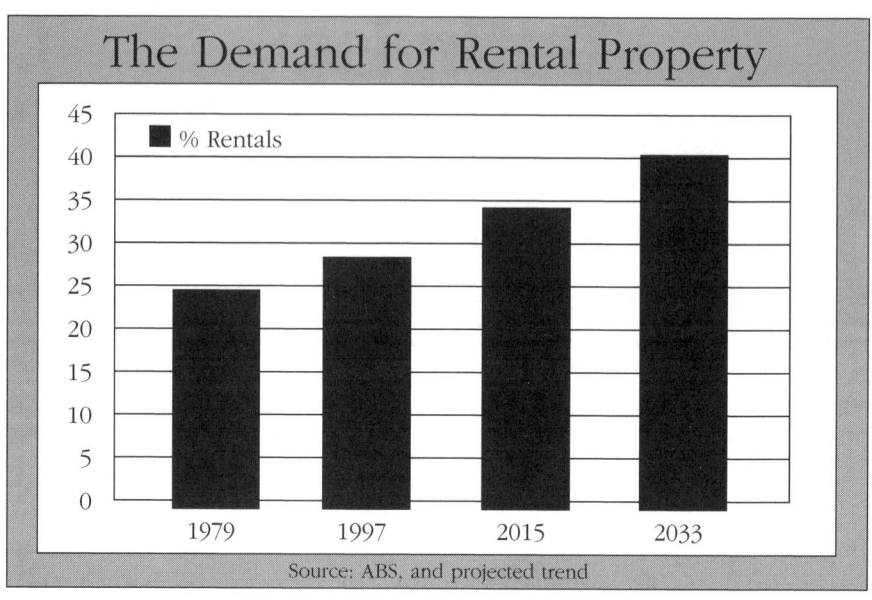

At the same time, the number of occupants per property is dropping – partly in line with the ageing population.

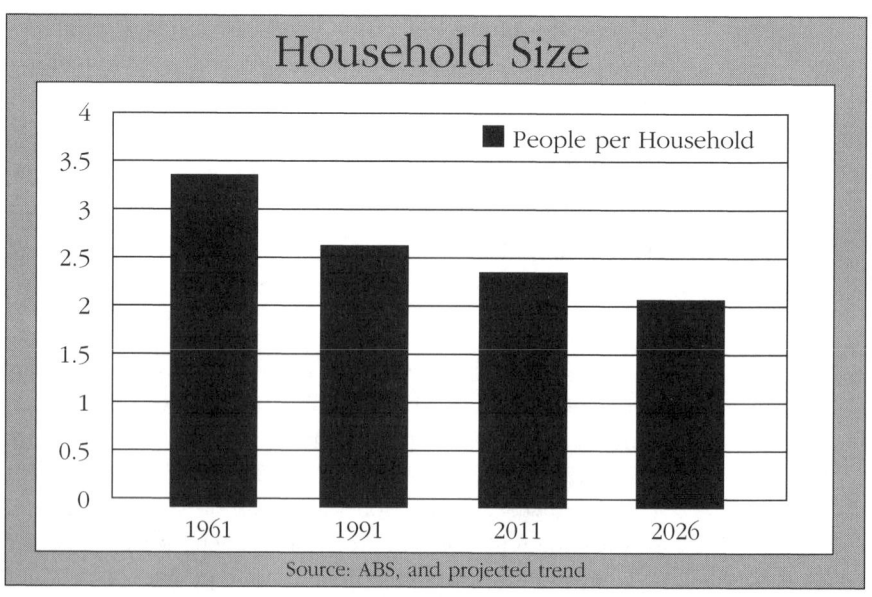

So we can safely project an increase in demand for rental property well into the 21st century.

There are many advantages to renting – although, of course, capital growth isn't one of them! Flexibility is a major factor, in view of increasing mobility and decreasing job security. Not having financial or managerial responsibility for a property is attractive to many people. And, as we noted in Chapter 1, a mortgage can seem like an unacceptable level of debt (if you don't look for the advantages of affordability, leverage and capital growth).

> We can safely project an increase in demand for rental property well into the 21st century.

One important thing to recognise, however, is that your market for tenants is principally made up of people in the lower income bracket. This is where the demand is. And to take advantage of that demand, we need to buy the kind of property that we can rent out at an affordable percentage of the average income. In other words: *aim for affordability* (Chapter 8). We'll come back to this a bit later, when we discuss the amount of rent we can charge.

OPTIMISING YOUR RENTAL INCOME

There are two ways you could theoretically go about optimising your rental income from a property:

- One is to maximise your income by charging the highest possible rent. If you charge the highest possible rent on the cheapest possible property, your margins look (in theory) particularly healthy.
- The other is to charge a moderate (even below-average) rent on a higher-priced property in a more popular residential area.

If you wanted to be greedy, you might think that the first option looked good. And you'd be shooting yourself in the foot.

Optimising rental income does not mean charging the *highest* rent: it means ensuring that the property attracts and retains tenants, and therefore maintains a *constant* rental income. The key is avoiding *vacancy,* which generates no income at all.

The two biggest factors in avoiding vacancy are:
- investing in an area with a high and preferably growing demand for rental property
- charging affordable, competitive rents.

Let's look at each of these in turn.

BEWARE 'BARGAINS'

We'll tackle the most common mistake first: it's a false economy to buy into a secondary suburb (high unemployment, low property values) because the property is 'cheap'. Property in a low-demand area may look like a bargain in pure purchase price terms, but it won't show a return in consistent rental income. (In property, a 'bargain' is just a way for someone to unload their problems onto you.)

We pinpointed Brisbane as a city currently showing significant population, employment and capital growth – and that's a step in the right direction but you *still* need to do your homework. You could buy a house in some parts of Logan City, for example, for $300,000, and a unit for $260,000. If that sounds like 'good value', look again: double-digit unemployment figures, high youth crime rates – and, not surprisingly, a lot of vacant property!

> In property, a 'bargain' is just a way for someone to unload their problems onto you...

The area has tripped up a lot of property investors over the last 20 years. Developers and marketers have recklessly sold property which was grossly overvalued in parts of Woodridge and Kingston (Logan City), mainly to interstate buyers. For many years, those buyers had *negative* capital growth – and if they sold prior to the last boom, they would have suffered a significant loss. If they held on, they would finally have come out in front – but nowhere near as well off as if they had done a little homework! Meanwhile, they would also have been struggling with low rental demand, and bearing the weekly cost of their borrowings. Cash flow nightmare.

This *doesn't* mean that rental property isn't a good investment. On the contrary – and despite a few urban myths – the rental market is growing steadily, and many people who rent do so through choice, even in the lower income brackets. What it *does* mean is that you need to do your homework on the location and type of rental property that will attract and retain consistent, rent-paying tenants!

WHERE DO FAMILIES WANT TO LIVE?

Remember the six main reasons why people choose to live in a particular area:

1. Proximity to schools
2. Security (that is, safety) for the family
3. Adequate public transport
4. Proximity to shops
5. Availability of (or proximity to) employment
6. Recreational facilities

These factors match my criteria for location-for-capital-growth and my own survey of Brisbane rentals. They don't seem to have changed at all over the last 30 years. In fact, they make pretty good sense – and are a useful guide to the kind of residential area that sustains a high demand for rental property.

Choose a property where at least the top three of these six factors are present within a radius of, say, 3 km: you'll not only be able to maintain a steady rental income, but capital growth as well.

Another factor is the *type* of property renters look for.

Even if you aren't thinking of resale values and capital growth, based on land content (as discussed in Chapter 4), you'd want to think twice about buying units for rental. If I remind you that only 6.1% of Australians owner-occupy units, you might be entitled to assume that everyone *rents* units. But the fact is that the *vacancy rate of units/townhouses is double that of houses in most areas:* in other words, more units lie empty and income-idle. Given affordability, that average Australian household of 2.6 people still prefers to live in detached housing.

Another tip: don't buy in *complexes* with multiple properties for sale to investors.

- You will be competing for tenants with all the other investor-landlords.

- Since owner-occupiers prefer areas with fewer rental properties, you will be limiting your property's sell-on potential – and hence your capital growth. Invest in suburbs with no more than 35% of homes occupied by renters. (Again, this weighs heavily against units, which are overwhelmingly renter-occupied.)

We've already mentioned, briefly, another good, practical yardstick for assessing the demand for rental property in a particular area: *vacancy factor.* Let's look at it in more detail.

VACANCY FACTOR

The rental vacancy factor is the percentage of the total rental properties in a particular area that are vacant at any given time. It is a pretty fair reflection of demand for rental property in that area – and therefore a barometer of how consistent your rental income will be.

The easiest and most accurate way of determining the vacancy factor in an area you are interested in is to contact a couple of the local real estate agents and simply ask them:

- how many rental properties they have on their books (in total)
- how many of them are vacant at the moment.

Personally, I won't invest in an area where the rental vacancy factor is higher than 3%. This needs to be reassessed on a suburb by suburb basis, as cities can vary from 1–20%.

The following table shows the average rental vacancy factors across Australia, as compiled by the Real Estate Institute of Australia.

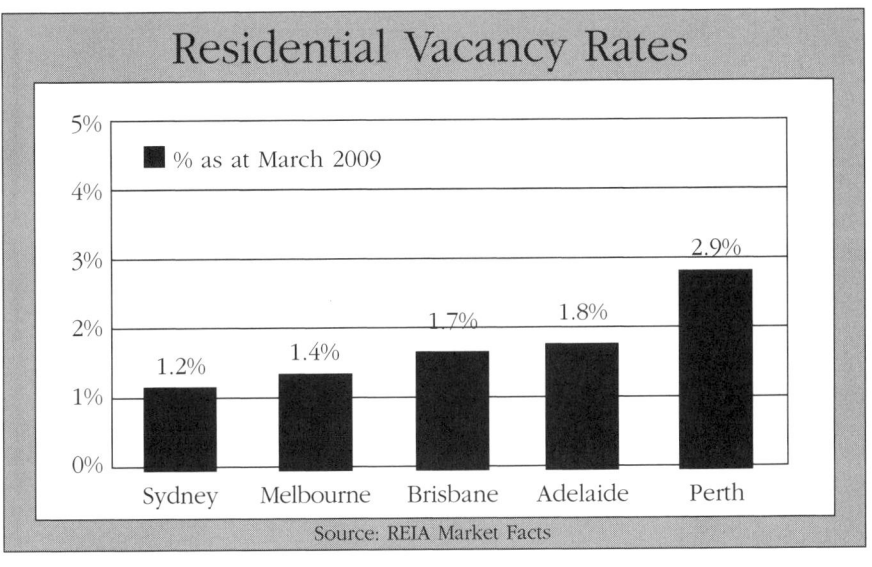

Chapter 5 - *Optimise your income*

This is a useful exercise in interpreting available information. The Real Estate Institutes' data can give a false perspective on vacancy rates: the figures may include units *and* housing, disguising the risks and opportunities. For example, in Melbourne, the vacancy rate for units could be 9–10% – while housing may only be 1–2%: risks in units, opportunities in houses. Similarly, you'll need to look at the position suburb by suburb: some are vastly over-supplied with rental properties, and so have much higher vacancy rates than others where there is still demand. Sorry – but I did warn you at the outset of the book that you'd have to do your homework!

WHAT RENT SHOULD YOU CHARGE?

If your property is empty, it is income-idle. If you want to maintain a constant income, you need to secure a constant supply of tenants. One good way of doing this is to check the suitability and vacancy factor of an area before you buy. Another is to avoid being greedy about rent.

Buy rental property on which the market rate of rent is *no more than 30% of the average household's disposable income:* that makes it affordable to most people with a job. If disposable income is around $1,000 per week, $300 per week is an affordable rent.

The following table shows average incomes in different states. I use it as a barometer for buying, and setting rent on properties. It's one of those 'changeable weather patterns' I mentioned in the Introduction to this book, and requires on-going monitoring, as part of the basic discipline of wealth building.

Capital City Rental Affordability

	Sydney	Melbourne	Brisbane	Adelaide	Perth
Average Weekly Earnings	$1,981	$1,734	$1,941	$1,473	$1,821
Recommended Affordable Rental*	$594	$520	$582	$442	$546

* Based on 30% of average weekly ordinary time earnings
Source: ABS October 2009

Over the years, I have also made a point of renting my property around 5% *below* the going market rate. That way, if I advertise a house on Saturday, by Sunday afternoon I will have it rented to the tenant of my choice. At a cost of just $10 –$15 per week, I have avoided competition with most other rental properties advertised, ensured minimal vacant time, and had a number of applicants to choose from. Because I tend to acquire property at the low end of the range, my rents tend to be around $350 per week which is highly affordable and attractive.

> **Even three weeks is a long period to have to pay the mortgage without the support of rental income.**

I see a lot of investors trying the opposite strategy, hanging out for the market rental value of their property, or more. For the sake of $5 or $10 per week, they might wait 4–6 weeks during which the property is vacant – and in the end, settle for any tenant who comes along, increasing the risk of rapid tenant turnover – or worse. Even three weeks is a long period to have to pay the mortgage without the support of rental income.

The other temptation is for higher-income earners to buy expensive property and charge higher rents, thinking that – since they have more money – they should invest in a higher-priced property: it *must* be less hassle than two smaller properties. Not necessarily – and not the best way to build wealth. (We'll discuss this in more detail in Chapter 8.)

If your income is to pull its weight in offsetting your outlays, as our structure suggests, you will have to increase your rents from time-to-time in line with inflation. But if you have set a discounted rent in the first place, and if you have invested in an area with high and growing rental demand, this shouldn't be a problem.

Case example

In 1987–88, I acquired over 30 rental properties in the regional town of Gladstone (south of Mackay), prior to commitment by Queensland government and industry to over a billion dollars in capital works projects in the area. I spoke to the real estate agent about the total number of properties he had under management: more than 400 at the time, including the ones I had acquired. And he hardly had a vacancy.

I couldn't understand why the rents were hovering at around $55–65 per week - and had been, for the best part of 6–7 years, in a high-inflation environment. The agent's answer was that he couldn't justify a rent increase – and when I told him I was proposing to increase my tenants' rent, he swore flat out that they simply wouldn't pay it. I went ahead and increased the average rent from $65 per week to $120 per week – and still did not have a single property vacant for more than two weeks at a time.

The moral of the story is: if you choose a high-demand, low-vacancy area, you will always have tenants, and you will be able to increase rents in my experience by 8% per annum (or a percentage of the property's value) over the entire period of your ownership.

Post script: *I got out of Gladstone in 1989. Remember the vulnerability of regional markets (Chapter 4)? The promised investment in the city never came to fruition, and real estate prices have remained flat there for almost nine years. Chalk it up as one of my mistakes.*

RENTAL? BUT THAT MEANS TENANTS!

This is another one of those areas where emotion tends to overtake logic. We've all heard the horror stories of bikie gangs inhabiting a property, 10 people to a room, all but demolishing the house, never paying the rent, and leaving their luckless landlord with huge repair bills, a mortgage to service and eviction notices to draw up.

OK, there are 'problem' tenants. (In fact, mostly there are 'tenants with problems', which is not quite the same thing.) Some problems can be avoided, and others can be overcome.

☑ **Set rents just below the market rate**

This gives you greater discretion in choosing your tenants. It increases the likelihood that they will be able to continue to afford the rent. It also creates a degree of loyalty – and I find that tenants are more willing to look after the property and use their own initiative (and even money) to make small repairs and replacements, knowing that their landlord is helping them out a little.

At the end of the day, $10 per week off your bottom line income is a small price to pay for a comparatively hassle-free tenancy – particularly by the time you are the landlord of four or five properties.

$10 per week off your bottom line income is a small price to pay for a comparatively hassle-free tenancy.

☑ **Check out prospective tenants the way you would a prospective employee**

When the agents who manage my property tell me that they have a new tenant for it, I want to know:
- Have they got a job, and how long have they been at that job? Does the employer back this up?
- Where have they lived for the last five years? Did they pay the rent? Was the bond refunded in full? Does the previous landlord back this up?

These two checks alone will weed out most potential bad tenants. You really do need to know the answer to these questions before you can rent a property – just like getting references from somebody you might consider employing. Potential good tenants won't mind being asked.

We've reproduced our Tenancy Application form at the end of this chapter, if you're interested in the details.

☑ Cover the costs of the unexpected

People lose jobs, relationships break up, things happen.

Fortunately, there are insurance policies for almost everything, including some specifically tailored to rental properties. You can insure against financial loss – for example, by a tenant defaulting on rent or leaving without notice – if the outstanding amount is not already covered by the bond. You can insure the building and its contents against accidental damage, fire, theft, and malicious damage by the tenant. (The latter is actually pretty rare, despite the bikie gang stories!)

Do take out *Landlord Protection Insurance*. If you are buying a property for $400,000, on which the rent might be $400 per week, it will cost you around $255 per year (that's less than a weeks' rent) to take this insurance out. This will ensure that you will receive a full 52 weeks' rent per year. In fact, we insist that all Custodian clients take out such insurance.

If a tenant leaves without paying the rent or causes malicious damage, the necessary bills can still be paid. It is absolutely vital to your wealth building program that you *maintain your cash flow*: you can't afford to be late with interest payments, because banks charge penalties – sometimes 3–4% above their going rate.

I also set aside a *contingency fund* of two months' rent, plus the amount of the excess payable on any insurance claim: that's usually enough to give everybody some leeway.

Case example

Some time ago, I rented a property to a nice young couple, both with jobs. They were in a de facto relationship that had lasted for two years. Their jobs checked out, and the bond from their previous rental had been refunded in full. So far, so good. Unfortunately, the relationship hit the rocks, she moved out, he lost it, and then lost his job... Six weeks later (after I had evicted him), I found that he had used the ceiling in the third bedroom as an elaborate watering system for growing marijuana... The insurance covered $610. However, I had to fork out the money for repairs before the insurance company paid up – mainly so I could rent the property out again quickly: my policy didn't cover loss of rent. (In those days, I didn't worry about those things, but if I had had then the kind of policy I have now, the excess would only have been about $160... You live and learn.) As it was, the net cost to me was around $860 ($2000 in today's terms): about five weeks' rent.

> **If things can happen, they will – and usually all at the same time!**

In light of this story, my formula of two months' rent plus rental insurance excess may seem overly cautious, but if you are building a portfolio of five or six properties, it's best to operate under Murphy's Law: if things can happen, they will – and usually all at the same time!

☑ Get someone else to take on the management tasks – and hassles – for you

A professional managing agent can take everything out of your hands (if that's what you want): advertise the property; vet and select tenants; organise maintenance; handle finance; communicate with the tenants, local authorities and service providers; and so on. (Over the page, I've reproduced the form we use to ensure that agents vet our tenants effectively.)

Don't just give the property to *any* agent. As ever, look behind the veil. Make sure the agent is well established: a full-time property manager and a large rent roll with few vacancies are good signs. Ask the agent for a reference from some of his or her landlords. And please don't fall into the trap of going with the agent who offers you the most rent! Remember, higher rent can mean more hassles and longer vacancies.

CONCLUSION

Don't let words like 'problem', 'insurance' and 'eviction' put you off! Managing tenants is seldom as much of a hassle as you might fear – even if you choose to handle it yourself. And income from rent is the fuel for your capital growth.

Rental income on its own will not cover all your outlays on an investment property. But there's another source of income available from your investment property: paying less tax! We'll go on to talk about tax benefits in Chapter 6.

Tenancy Application [Sample]

APPLICANT ONE

Full Name: _____ D.O.B. _____
Present Address: _____ Phone: _____
Period of Occupancy: _____
Reason for Leaving: _____
Name of Agent or Owner: _____ Rent Paid: _____
Address: _____ Phone: _____
Previous Address: _____
Period of Occupancy: _____
Reason for Leaving: _____
Name of Agent or Owner: _____ Rent Paid: _____
Address: _____ Phone: _____
Car Registration Number: ___ Drivers Licence No: ___ State: ___
Name of person to contact in case of emergency: _____
Address: _____ Phone: _____

PERSONAL REFERENCES (Not a relative)

1. Name: _____
   Address: _____ Phone: _____
   Relationship: _____ How long known: _____
2. Name: _____
   Address: _____ Phone: _____
   Relationship: _____ How long known: _____

IF STUDENT

Name of College, TAFE or University: _____
Faculty / Course: _____
Student ID Number: _____

Source: Peter Campbell Realty

OCCUPATION

Current Occupation: _____
Current Employer : _____
Address: _____
Phone: _____ Period of Employment: _____
Income: $_____
If employed for less than 6 months – previous employer: ___
If Self Employed – Industry: _____ How Long: _____
Accountant: _____ Phone: _____

Full Name of other persons (including children) wishing to occupy the above premises other than the Applicants: (Please include ages of children)

_____

Pets Owned: _____
Breed: _____
Are they registered with any Council: YES / NO

1. Have you ever been evicted by a Landlord or Agent?
   YES / NO   If yes, give details: _____
2. Have you been refused another property by any Landlord or Agent?
   YES / NO   If yes, give details: _____
3. Are you in debt to another Agent or Landlord?
   YES / NO   If yes, give details: _____
4. Is there any reason known to you that would affect your rental payments?
   YES / NO   If yes, give details: _____

Chapter 5 - Optimise your income

DISCLAIMER / AUTHORITY

I, the said applicant, do solemnly and sincerely declare that the information contained in this application is true and correct and that all of the information was given of my own free will. I declare that I am not bankrupt. I further authorise the letting agent to contact and/or conduct any inquiries and/or searches with regard to the information and references supplied in this application.

I, the said applicant, do solemnly and sincerely declare:
I have inspected the property located at _____.
I have of my own accord decided that I wish to rent the aforementioned property commencing _____ for a period of ___ months and that the rental on the property is $ _____ per week and the bond amount to be paid is $ _____.
I have been informed, understand and agree that should this application not be accepted, the agent is not required to disclose why or supply any reason for the rejection of this application.

I have been informed, understand and agree that upon acceptance of this application, I will sign the appropriate paperwork and pay a minimum of one (1) week's rent within twenty four (24) hours of such acceptance. I have been informed, understand and agree that all monies are to be paid (being two (2) weeks' rent and bond) before commencement of the lease and collection of any keys to the property.

Privacy Act acknowledgement

In accordance with Section 18n of the Privacy Act, I authorise you to give information to and obtain information from all credit providers and references named in this application. I understand this can include information about my credit worthiness, credit standing, credit history or credit capacity. I understand this information may be used to assess my application.

Applicant one signature _____ Date _____

Applicant two signature _____ Date _____

NOTICE TO ALL RESIDENTIAL TENANCY APPLICANTS

Before any application will be considered, each applicant must achieve a minimum of 100 check points.

Last 4 Rent Receipts	50 Points
Drivers License	40 Points
Passport	40 Points
Photo ID	30 Points
Pension Card	20 Points
Minimum 2 references from previous Landlord / Agent	20 Points
Pay Advice	15 Points
References	10 Points (each)
Current Motor Vehicle Rego Papers	10 Points
Copy of previous Telephone, Electricity or Gas Account	10 Points (each)
Bank Statement	10 Points
Copy of Birth Certificate	10 Points

Should you not be able to meet the 100 check points, please speak to the property manager.

Notes

Chapter 6 [Step 3]
Maximise your tax benefits

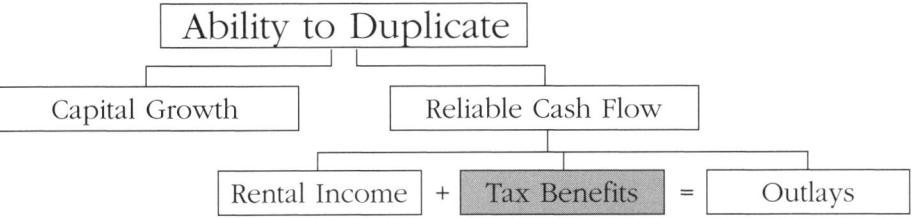

Alongside income, tax savings are the essential 'fuel' for building wealth. It is fundamental to our structure that we maximise our tax benefits, thereby ensuring that we have minimal cash outlays on our investment property – thereby, in turn, placing no significant restrictions on our ability to build our portfolio by reinvesting our increased equity.

This – at last! – is where 'negative gearing' comes in.

WHAT IS NEGATIVE GEARING?

Gearing is borrowing money for the purposes of investment – and we will be discussing how to get the most out of it in Chapter 7, on obtaining and using finance.

Negative gearing is the tax benefit that accrues when the income from an investment fails to cover the outlays on that investment, so that you are making a 'book loss', or negative income. (Don't panic: remember, the capital value of your asset is still growing.) A residential investment property would be negatively-geared if, for example, the mortgage interest and other tax-deductible items exceeded the rental income.

Definition

Negative gearing occurs when your total outlays to maintain an investment are greater than your income from the investment: the difference is claimable as a tax deduction.

The thing is, this loss – the difference between your outlays and your income – is *tax deductible*. It can be offset against your personal income (including salary) to reduce your taxable income, and perhaps even put you into a lower tax bracket. The upshot is that you *pay less tax* – and if that doesn't sound like a good idea, there's something pretty unusual about your thinking.

WHAT DEDUCTIONS CAN YOU CLAIM?

Here are some of the main cash deductions you can claim on any rental property.

- ☑ Loan interest. (Other borrowing costs – loan application and valuation fees, mortgage registration and insurance etc – are deductable over a period of time)
- ☑ Insurance premiums
- ☑ Fees – for example, for property/rental management, legal advice and accountancy (if you decide to get all these deductions drawn up by a professional. You could also pay your spouse a fee for keeping regular accounts on the property, and claim that! This may reduce your combined income tax bill!)
- ☑ Rates and local government charges
- ☑ Maintenance, repair and upkeep costs
- ☑ Sundry business expenses – like bank charges, stationery and travel (including reasonable inspections of property out of state)

Here's an example. Say you purchase a rental property for $400,000, borrowing 90% of the purchase price at 7% interest only, and you let it out at $350 per week for 50 weeks of the year, for an annual rental income of $17,500.

		Rental income $17,500
Deductions:	$	
Loan interest	25,200	
Insurance	430	
Maintenance	770	
Rates	1,400	
Rental management	1,540	
TOTAL ANNUAL CASH OUTLAY	29,340	
Borrowing costs	400	
TOTAL DEDUCTIONS	($29,740)	
Shortfall		($12,240)

That shortfall is deducted from your gross income – say, $60,000 – to give you a taxable income of $47,760. Here's the basic calculation based on the tax year 2010-2011:

		After deductions on property:	
Gross income:	$60,000	Taxable income:	$47,760
Tax payable:	$12,150	Tax payable:	$8294.40
Net after-tax income:	$47,850	Net after-tax income:	$39,465.60
		Tax saving:	$3,855.60

This example was based on your buying an older property – as 77% of investors who take advantage of negative gearing do. It doesn't offer much of a tax deduction, but it is a negatively geared asset, so you do get a tax saving.

THE DIFFERENCE THAT MAKES A DIFFERENCE: DEPRECIATION

The *depreciation of an asset used to produce income* is a non-cash deductible item. This means you can claim a percentage of the declining value of furniture, fixtures and fittings, over a number of years of wear and tear. But somewhere in that list of depreciating items – carpets, curtains, cupboards, cookers – is the biggest item of all: the building.

Here's the key: a residential building constructed after July 1985 that is used to produce income can be depreciated.

Construction commenced:	Claimable depreciation rate:	Over:
July 1985 – September 1987	4%	25 years
September 1987 onwards	2.5%	40 years

Depreciation on a new building can add up to thousands of dollars a year – and it's a 'non-cash' deduction, which means that you don't actually have to lay out any cash each year in order to claim the 'loss'! This is the factor that significantly reduces your taxable income – and your tax payments. It's what makes our *income + tax benefits ≃ outlays* structure work best.

Let's look at our example, supposing now that you bought a *new* rental property of the same value and on the same terms.

Rental income $17,500

	$	
TOTAL ANNUAL CASH OUTLAY	29,340	
NON-CASH COSTS		
Borrowing costs	400	
Depreciation	6,000	
TOTAL DEDUCTIONS	($35,740)	
Shortfall		($18,240)

Your taxable income is now ($60,000 - $18,240) = $41,760.

And here's the new tax calculation:

After deductions on new property:

Gross income:	$60,000	Taxable income:	$41,760
Tax payable:	$12,150	Tax payable:	$ 6404.40
Net after-tax income:	$47,850	Net after-tax income:	$35,355.60

Your tax has been reduced by $5745.60

And think of it purely in cash flow terms:

Investment Cash Flow

	$	
Rental income	17,500	per annum
Cash outlays	(29,340)	per annum
Cash shortfall	(11,840)	per annum
Tax benefit (after non-cash deductions)	5,745.60	per annum
After tax cost	6,094.40	

Cost per week: $117.20

This allows you an earlier opportunity to add onto your portfolio without eating too much into your personal cash flow. And our example only shows one property: multiply the effect by five or six.

It's all about *cash flow management.* You've got the opportunity to write off the construction value of the house and fittings over the years, leaving only the bare land value – which is the part of your investment that's going to go up in value. The components of your house and land package should add up something like this:

Total purchase price	$400,000
Land	$200,000
House (structure)	$180,000
Fittings	$20,000

You can write off the fittings over the first five years, which is a major boost to your income, and to your ability to add on to your portfolio during that period. That's efficient cash flow management, and efficient wealth building.

In order to maximise your depreciation, you'll need a *quantity surveyor's report*. A lot of investors and even accountants think that depreciation is 2.5% of the value of the building. In fact, if the building is new, you can get a quantity surveyor to separate the fixtures and fittings from the building structure and claim 'accelerated depreciation' – perhaps 10–20% per annum – on the fixtures and fittings. This offers useful additional cash flow for your first five years of ownership, until your rent grows to the point where you become cash flow positive. It's a completely legitimate 'trick' of the trade that all investors should be taking advantage of.

WHO WANTS TO PAY MORE TAX THAN THEY HAVE TO?

I know the maths can be a bit mind boggling – but it's not essential to do all the sums at this stage. (Once you get into negatively-geared investments, it's a good idea, in any case, to have your tax return completed by a competent accountant or tax adviser, so that you are sure to claim all your legitimate deductions.)

But here's the bottom line. Am I really saying that by claiming a 'book loss', you can not only cover the shortfall – but actually walk away with extra cash in your pay packet? That's exactly what I'm saying.

At the moment, if you are on a salary of $100,000, you may have to work Monday and part of Tuesday of each week *just to pay the tax!*

> Am I saying that you can actually walk away with extra cash in your pay packet? That's exactly what I'm saying.

Some people think about buying older properties for investment purposes

Negative gearing allows you to legitimately minimise the amount of tax you pay – as well as fuelling capital growth. Negatively-geared rental property is one of the most tax-efficient investment vehicles available.

If you are a PAYG Income Tax payer, and your deductions are more than $500 or 10% of your gross salary (whichever is greater) for the year, you don't even have to wait for an end-of-year refund: you can claim an immediate adjustment to the tax that is deducted from your salary at source by your employer. Section 15.15 (Schedule 1) of the *Tax Administration Act 1953* provides for this PAYG Income Tax Withholding adjustment and the form used to claim for it is called a PAYG Income Tax Withholding Variation (ITWV) Application.

Anybody on PAYG Income Tax Withholding ought to look into this! The higher your income – and your marginal tax rate – the more tax you can save.

AND HOW *DO* AUSTRALIANS INVEST?

Let's complete the grim picture.

34% BUY UNITS
26% BUY IN THEIR OWN POSTCODE
ONLY 3% MAXIMISE THEIR TAX BENEFITS

NEED ANY FURTHER INCENTIVES?

There are a couple of other little gems hidden in the fine print of the *Income Tax Administration Act 1997*, which can also improve your bottom line.

- Under Section 8.1, you may be able to claim payment of a reasonable sum (reflecting time and effort spent) to your spouse, a friend, or other nominated person, as a fee for managing the books of your rental property. (We call this 'grocery money'.) This may reduce the combined tax bill of the individuals.

- Another 'perk' in owning properties interstate is that you can travel to see them twice a year (and take your book-keeper) – and deduct the full cost of the travel, as well as one night's accommodation, while you inspect your property and meet with the agent. (This is something we'd encourage you to do anyway – but beware of staying a few extra days. To obtain a full tax deduction, the sole purpose of the trip must be to inspect the property.)

POSITIVE THINKING
FOR NEGATIVE GEARING

Quite bluntly, if you buy a house built before 1985 as an investment property, you need your head read! Why would you do it?

A lot of investors acquire older properties, because they think they are 'better value' (they can save an extra $5,000 or $10,000 on the purchase price) and of course

This isn't your home we're talking about, it's a negatively-geared asset.

they 'prefer the feel' of an older house. But – at the risk of repeating myself – it is the *land* that appreciates in value: the house is only the vehicle by which we can generate rental income and qualify for tax deductions, so that we can offset our cash outlays while we achieve capital growth.

It really doesn't matter if we pay a little bit extra for a newer property: it will more than pay for itself via a substantial tax rebate. And sorry, but it *really* doesn't matter if you 'like' an old house: this isn't your home we're talking about, it's a negatively-geared asset to offset your tax and maximise your income. Logic – not emotion – for capital growth.

Remember our structure: that's what cash flow management and negative gearing are all about. Using the figures from our example on page 105:

Case example

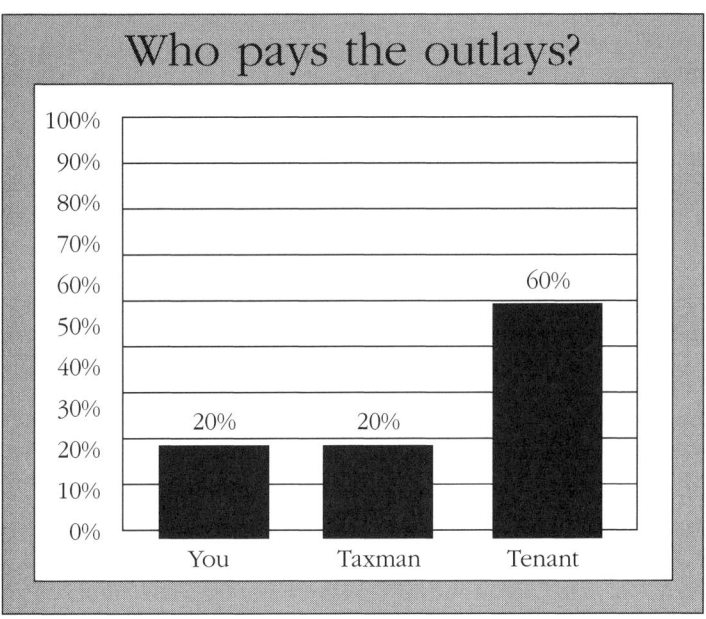

The following table shows the real value of buying new versus old.

	New (Newly-built house)	Old (5-year-old comparable)
	$	$
Price	400,000	375,000
Land Value	200,000	200,000
Building	200,000	175,000
Depreciable amount	200,000	154,000
'Real' purchase price (for the land)	200,000	221,000

Often you'll see a new house priced at $400,000, with a five-year-old (otherwise comparable) house next door for sale at $375,000. Most investors would buy the five-year-old house thinking it was a better investment – perhaps even jumping to the conclusion that they had found the 'worst house in the best street'.

But look beneath the surface of the asset: what is its real depreciable value to you? In the case of the brand new home you can write off the total amount of the building – so you're effectively paying for the key asset (the land) exactly what it's really worth. In the case of the five-year-old home, you can only write off perhaps 85% of the building value – leaving you paying more than the land's true value.

Depreciation is a key factor that will help you identify the intrinsic value of a property asset: in other words, the value of the *land* – since that's the commodity that is going to appreciate in value.

Food for thought?

Chapter 7
Finance
to build

[Step 4]

In Chapter 3, we saw that building a portfolio is based on gearing, and the way it can be leveraged when you buy residential real estate, so that you can:

- minimise your initial capital input into the investment (10% equity)
- use the bank's money – in effect – to build wealth (90% borrowing)
- reap 100% per annum return on your capital
- offset your costs with rental income and the tax benefits of negative gearing
- use equity growth to provide start-up equity for subsequent acquisitions by duplicating the process.

I trust that, by now, all that sounds pretty straight forward! (If it doesn't: don't worry. Really. As you investigate further, and still more as you begin to work the system, it will all fall into place as far as it needs to.)

In this chapter, we look at some of the practical issues around gearing: property values and valuations, choosing and using loan providers, and evaluating different finance options.

ASSESSING THE VALUE OF YOUR PROPERTY

It's vital for you to be able to make a basic assessment of the value of a property, so that you can check that you are paying a fair price.

The key to the valuation – and capital growth – of your property will (as ever) be the land.

One simple method of determining the value of your investment is to divide it into two components: the land value, and the replacement cost of the building.

For a house, this is quite simple: you can usually estimate the *land value* by sales of comparable vacant land sites. This information can be obtained from the Valuer General's Office in the appropriate state department. (For example, in Queensland, it is the Department of Environment and Resource Management, in New South Wales, it is the Land and Property Management Authority, in Victoria, it is the Department of Sustainability and Environment and in Western Australia, it is the Department of Commerce.) You just have to request a sales report of all residential allotments within a recent period. (Alternatively, *rates notices* include 'unimproved land values'.) Another easy method is to ask the real estate agent or developer about the land component of a property. In a new estate, this is pretty straightforward, and you should also get some forecasts of future development and projected land values, as an indication of how your equity might increase over time.

The other component is the *replacement cost* of the house. You can estimate this by a simple formula:

Total size of house (square metres) x $ rate per square metre

Builders aren't always eager to give out rates per metre, but in most capital cities you can find project homes advertised in the newspapers, with a reasonable range of standard building rates — from $1000–1,500 per square metre. This doesn't include footings, so add on another $100 per square metre for footings and earthworks, and then have a quantity surveyor identify the value of your fixtures and fittings, as well as landscaping. (In any case, it's a good idea to get a quantity surveyor's valuation when you are claiming tax deductions for depreciation, as discussed in chapter 6 – and for $400–500, this is a useful cross-check.)

The other method of assessing a property's value is simply looking at *comparable sales*. However, this is an inaccurate approach at best, and can be deceptive. You don't know the circumstances of the purchaser or vendor, which may have distorted the price. In the case of blocks of units, they may have been sold with incentives, or to non-resident owners who didn't bother to check out the value beneath the price tag – with the result that few owners have actually paid anything resembling replacement cost. I prefer to do a search with the relevant state's Valuer General's Office, checking sales over the previous six months where the purchaser's address coincides with the property sold: that is, where the owner is a resident.

BANK VALUATIONS

The dynamic of equity growth (using interest-only loans) is that the debt stays constant, while the value of the property goes up. But who defines the 'value' part of that equation?

> **Bank valuations can be deceptive – and potentially disastrous.**

For the purposes of assessing equity, the only valuation that matters is the one adopted by the bank that is lending you the balance of the acquisition costs.

Ideally, the value used by your lender should be the same as the purchase price, or more.

If the bank valuation is significantly lower than the purchase price (and therefore the amount of the loan), the bank may protect itself by writing down the security value of the property – and this can affect your total equity position with that bank. Unfortunately, this is not a rare occurrence: bank valuations can be deceptive – and potentially disastrous.

Let's say your home is worth $400,000, and you have a debt with the bank of $120,000.

You apply to buy a new investment property, priced at $300,000: you decide to use the equity from your home, and roll the loans together into a single loan package, which allows you to borrow 100% of the purchase price, plus costs. (This is called *zero-cost financing*, which we'll discuss further, a bit later in the chapter.) However, the bank's valuation of your investment property – undisclosed to you – is only $280,000. Here's what happens.

Own home:	House value	$400,000
	Borrowed	$120,000
	Equity	$280,000
		(70%)
Investment property:	Purchase price	$300,000
	Costs	$15,000
	Borrow	$315,000
	Bank valuation	$280,000
Total security value of assets (house value + bank's valuation of investment property):		$680,000
Total borrowings:		$435,000
	Equity:	$245,000
		(36%)

Your equity has plunged from 70% to 36%, and your net assets from $280,000 to $245,000 – according to the bank. And you're not unique: this happens depressingly often. People purchase all types of investment property – from high-rise units to town house units and houses – at over-inflated prices: anything from $30,000 to $100,000 over the bank's appraisal of the property's security value.

Frankly, I think it's outrageous that banks continue to do this sort of thing. If they aren't prepared to disclose their valuer's appraisal of the security value of the investment property, their loan should be limited to the amount of their valuation. It could take investors 5–10 years to recoup their lost capital as a result of a wide differential!

Caveat emptor: buyer, beware. To ensure you don't get caught out on this:

- Avoid *'cross-collateralisation'*, where the lender uses *all* properties mortgaged as security for your outstanding loans. You need to find a lender who will advance the highest proportion of the property's purchase (a high loan value ratio or LVR) *without* requiring the use of *another* property – or the family home – as additional collateral.

    In other words, take out a *separate loan* for your investment property.

- Watch out for *'all monies' clauses,* whereby the lender is allowed to secure 'any' outstanding loans you have with them (home loan, credit card, personal loan, overdraft and so on) against the value of the mortgaged property – whether they have advised you of this directly or not.

    This may mean financing your investment property with a *different lender* to the one that holds the mortgage on the family home and other accounts.

This gives you added protection, should there be a problem with your investment portfolio (or your own credit cards) at any time, since your home isn't tied up with your investment.

You can still use the equity in your own home effectively, by simply applying to your home loan bank for the 10% deposit on your first investment property.

In any case, find a lender who is prepared to disclose the security value of the property you are acquiring. If you are acquiring it through an agent and using a finance broker, obtain a copy of the valuation. Ensure that it equals your purchase price or comes within, say, 5% of it. (I must admit that I have often had to settle for an assessment that didn't quite meet my price. Read on, and you'll know why.)

VALUERS

Given that it is the bank's perception of the value of the property that matters, you'd hope to be able to have confidence in the people they get to do the valuations. Nice idea.

Banks will often instruct panel valuers to value the property – and some of the most frustrating experiences I've had in real estate investment over the years have been dealings with these self-styled 'experts' in property. Valuations are not, at the best of times, an exact science. The banks use valuers because they have an insurance indemnity: if an investor defaults, and it is found that the property valuation was not representative of market values at the time of purchase, the bank can claim against the valuer.

I, personally, have seen the same property valued by three different valuers, where the highest valuation was double the lowest!

The big valuation firms tend to have young valuers, in their twenties, doing 10-15 valuations a day – which doesn't make for the most painstaking research. They will search an area, through the Valuer General's Office, and find a benchmark, or range of sales. The Valuer General's sales records are three to six months old, so if the market is really moving, it may not be reflected by the valuation. Moreover, the valuers will often

> Given that it is the bank's perception of the value of the property that matters, you'd hope to be able to have confidence in the people they get to do the valuations. Nice idea.

use the *lowest* comparable sale price for your purchase – because their instructions from the bank are to supply a value at which the property would sell in the local market within three months. (This may vary if you have been required to take out mortgage insurance.)

Valuers will quite openly admit that if they were valuing a property for *you* – as opposed to the bank – they might strike a higher valuation figure. As it is, they are bound to be conservative.

So the valuation may well be a little under your price – but anything over 5% is a worry. Don't forget: this is the basis of the bank's assessment of your net equity!

Once again: do the homework. (Preferably, yourself.) Find comparable sales *to locals* – not out-of-state speculators – and if you can't: *don't buy.*

The point is: don't expect too much from valuers – but remember that the banks will rely on them. You need to work with them in order to secure equity growth and build a property portfolio. It's a good idea to:

- Establish a relationship with the bank-appointed valuer yourself, so you understand his or her methodology in carrying out the initial valuation of a property. Don't be afraid to argue the point. (As I mentioned above, most busy valuers are *so* busy that they tend to be conservative – but I've also seen them accept good, up-to-date evidence and change their initial appraisal.)

- Ask that valuer to revisit your property, once you become aware that there may have been some increase in values, and on a six- to twelve-month basis.

If you are going to appoint your own valuers, check that they will be acceptable to your bank. This way, you have access to the valuation information – and you know that this valuer's appraisal will be accepted by the bank.

CHOOSING A LOAN PROVIDER

Selecting the right source of finance for your investment portfolio will be integral to your capacity to build wealth.

This is another one of those decisions that needs to be made on logic, not emotion. Don't get sentimental about banks. Don't feel you have to be loyal to a bank – even if it's a big name, it sponsors your favourite sporting event, it already holds your account or home loan, and the staff are friendly at your local branch! With banks, loyalty only goes one way: they are uncaring at best – and at worst, they can be incompetent or manipulative, or both.

Remember our muscle-building analogy in Chapter 3? If finance corresponds to the carbohydrates that fuel your exercise, the lender is merely the brand of cereal or bread you choose to provide those carbohydrates. If you don't like the flavour of one – switch to another. Fortunately, competition is increasing within – and from outside – the bank sector, and you should be able to find a lender willing to accommodate you, if you shop around.

> **Don't get sentimental about banks.**

So what is a logical way of selecting and dealing with a loan provider? Here are a few of the major considerations:

- ✓ You need to establish with the bank from the outset that you intend to use the increased equity on the property to build an investment portfolio. Most of the important questions and decisions flow from there.

- ✓ Banks lend against security. You need to know the bank's loan value ratio (LVR) – what percentage it will lend on investment property. Some banks only lend 60% of valuation (or contract price), and others 90%. You are looking for a bank that will accept a 10% equity position.

Because, under our structure, most of your outlays are being met, you can afford to borrow 90% – and then, as soon as your first property increases in value by 10%, you should have enough equity with that bank to acquire a second property (and so on). If a bank requires 20% equity, it will take you twice as long to build a portfolio – with that particular bank.

Also, be aware that over time, the bank may move the goal posts on their lending criteria. This may be your signal to change banks...

✓ Find a lender who will give a high LVR *without cross-collateralisation*: requiring the use of another property (eg. the family home) as additional security. This protects your equity in other properties if there is a problem with one (as discussed earlier).

This may be a signal to change your lender

- ☑ For a loan of over 80%, you will be required to take out *mortgage insurance*, to cover the lender against potential losses if you default. (This is a once-only payment, and tax deductible over a period of time.) The main insurers – Genworth or QBE – may call for an independent valuation, so it is a good idea to ensure that the bank's valuer is on the mortgage valuation panel as well.

- ☑ Banks also lend against your anticipated ability to service the debt: that is, to maintain repayments. The *affordability* of the loan is calculated by total repayments (of all loans, credit card debts and so on) as a percentage of your gross income. Most banks are comfortable with 30–35%, but the figure can go as low as 25% and as high as 60%: shop around. I look for a bank that will do 40%.

- ☑ Also, aim for 80% of the projected rental income from the investment property to be included in your income for credit assessment, and for the tax savings on negative gearing to be taken into account: different banks calculate this in different ways, and it can make a big difference to how much you can borrow.

- ☑ The bank must be prepared to *disclose its appraisal of the security value* of the property, for comparison with the purchase price.

- ☑ Check for unnecessary or hidden *fees:* loan application fees, valuation fees, penalties for paying out (including refinancing) early, administration charges and so on.

- ☑ The bank must be flexible about *revisiting valuations*. Property, roughly speaking, doubles in value every 8–10 years, but within that trend there are constant fluctuations: you need to be checking comparable sales for signs of rising values – and the increased equity that you can use to increase your portfolio. Some of the major banks are less inclined to consider a revised valuation within 12 months of acquisition.

✓ Remember to consider the effect of *'all monies'* clauses: you may want to finance your investment property with a different lender to the one who holds your other accounts.

I have compiled a table of investment banks, what they will lend, and options for building a portfolio.

Major Financial Institutions' Lending Guidelines

Bank	Application fee	Annual ongoing fee	Mortgage insurance fee as % of loan	LVR	Value disclosure	Revalue in 12 months
Westpac	$750	$96	1.87%	90	No	No policy
CBA	$750	$96	1.87%	90	No	No policy
ANZ	$600	$60	1.87%	90	No	No policy
St George	$700	$120	1.87%	90	No	No policy
Suncorp	$600	$120	1.87%	90	No	No policy
Homeside	$762.50	$120	1.87%	90	No	No policy
RAMS	$895	Nil	1.87%	90	No	No policy
Aussie Home Loans	$500	Nil	1.87%	90	No	No policy

Each deal is assessed on a case-by-case basis.
Source: Investloan

As you can see, none of the banks currently disclose valuations and they have no policy on revisiting valuations inside of 12 months. You will need to monitor such policies, and push for their relaxation, if you are going to make the structure work – but you will find more flexibility among second-tier banks than among the Big Four.

Loans are also available from some of the major insurance companies and credit unions, or through a mortgage broker (for a fee), but frankly, it is the second-tier banks that are going to be most useful to you in building your property portfolio. Again, shop around. It may be worth paying an extra 0.25–0.50% in interest rates to find a lender who is prepared to support you in building a portfolio over time.

Chapter 7 - Finance to build | *121*

Be prepared to negotiate the interest rate. Indicate your intentions and ask questions. You might be able to obtain pre-approval at the time of your first acquisition.

Using a broker

There are some big advantages in using a finance broker to shop around for a deal for you. If you go to a major broker, they can often get you a better deal with your own bank than you could get by going direct to your bank manager. (Sad, isn't it?) Some of these brokers are doing $100–200 million worth of financing per month – and the banks are happy to pay them commissions and trail fees (a percentage of your interest for the life of the loan) in order to secure the business.

Your first port of call might naturally have been your local bank manager (who after all has probably been knocking on your door, wanting to lend you money). But if you are using your home as part of the equity, it could be harder than pulling sharks' teeth to get your home mortgage released from your investment portfolio (which has got to be your short-term goal). Local bank managers tend not to like this idea, because their security is better served by holding the deed to your home – but a broker has the negotiating power to represent *your* interests.

> A major broker can often get you a better deal with your own bank than you could. (Sad, isn't it?)

Some of the smaller brokers charge a fee for their service, but if you are going to use a broker, I would in any case recommend one of the larger ones, who have got the turnover – and therefore the negotiating power – to get you the best deal. Test them out and get them to offer you financing through a couple of banks on the terms and conditions you want – including having the valuation disclosed *and* the option to use equity in six to twelve months to repurchase.

Ten years ago, I set up Investloan, my own brokerage business, because I was frustrated with the banks and I could not find a broker to represent my interests. You can check them out if you are not getting anywhere with your bank or broker (www.investloan.com.au).

CHOOSING A FINANCE OPTION

Zero-cost financing

This is really just a fancy term for using the equity in your own home as collateral security for your investment property, instead of having to find a cash deposit. (We gave one example of how this could be done, earlier, emphasising that the bank's valuation must be the same as the purchase price.) This can be highly tax effective, as all your costs of acquiring the *investment* property, and the interest costs of the loan, can be deducted from your income tax. The repayments on your *home* are not similarly tax deductible. So if you do have spare cash, you are far better off using it to pay off your existing home mortgage and, in effect, using the equity that generates to borrow 100–110% on your investment property! Let's look at some numbers.

Home value	$400,000
Outstanding debt	$120,000
Value of investment property	$300,000
Stamp duty, legal/finance costs etc	$ 15,000
Total acquisition costs	$315,000
Total assets (bank's valuation)	$700,000
Total debt	$435,000
Of which:	
Investment debt (tax deductible)	$315,000

Chapter 7 - **Finance to build** | 123

Your goal should be to try to divert as much of your taxable income into your wealth building program as possible – using all legal opportunities available to you – in order to minimise your tax.

Interest only loans

Maximum tax deductions are based on interest only loans, as opposed to principal and interest (P & I) loans, because only *interest* payments are tax deductible.

Banks aren't always enthusiastic about this, as they prefer some principal to be paid off, but as you've probably gathered, by now, wealth building is about *managing your cash flow:* where you have an opportunity to minimise your cash outlays, do it. This will allow you to build earlier. (If you have any spare cash, use it to pay off the principal on your home loan.)

If you took a P & I loan for $150,000 over 25 years, in the first five years you would repay $13,257, or about 9% of the loan. This would affect your cash flow by $51 per week (in after tax dollars). It's also money that could otherwise have been ploughed back into wealth building.

Locking in a rate of interest

The most important thing in wealth building (if I may say it just one more time) is to manage our cash flow – not to get the highest rent, *nor the lowest interest rate.* My advice is to lock in your loan at the best rate you can find, for as long as you can.

You don't have to be in the business of interest rate forecasting to do this – although there are hundreds of economists and pseudo-economists who will offer you the crystal ball. If interest rates are at 7% and you can lock in for five years, do it: it's not going to be of tremendous consequence if they fall to 6%. You were happy with 7%: live with it.

As a worst case scenario, if you are locked in at 7% for five years, you could come out of the lock-in period with interest rates at 10%. But as interest rates increase, so do rents, and so too do the values of properties. (Surprisingly, demand also seems to remain high. In 1988–89, for example, interest rates went as high as 17% and there was a market frenzy such as I'd never seen.)

GEARING IN ACTION

Under our structure, you use the equity in your house, or put forward a cash deposit, for 10% of the purchase price of a new residential investment property which – thanks to rental income and negative gearing – thereafter partly pays for itself. When the value of the property has increased by 10%, you should have enough equity with the bank that loaned you the balance (assuming it is prepared to maintain a 10% equity position) to acquire a second investment property. You now have two assets working for you, both increasing in value and enabling you – in a shorter period of time – to build up further equity, to acquire your third property and so on.

Once you've acquired your second property, you are already in the charmed realm of the top individual investors.

- 87% acquire only one property
- 13% acquire more than one property
- Less than 1.5% acquire more than four properties

There will obviously be a limit to how many properties you can acquire over a given period of time – depending on your income, the rate of equity growth, and the amount of money your investment bank is prepared to lend you to build a portfolio. Discuss these things with a few prospective lenders. Remember, you can start small – and think big. It's not a race. Finance to build.

Notes

Chapter 8
Aim for affordability

[Step 5]

As I travel around Australia talking about wealth building and residential real estate, I find that almost everybody is prepared to get excited about land appreciating (for capital growth) and buildings depreciating (for negative gearing), and about maximising income and reducing tax. There are always a few doubts, concerns and 'what if?' questions (which I address in Chapter 11), but there's only one really big 'yes but...' And that's the dreaded Real Estate Cycle.

Booms and busts. Upturns and downturns. Height of the market, depth of the recession. What happens if you buy or sell at the wrong time or at the wrong price?

Let's get some perspective about this.

UPS AND DOWNS

The idea of economic cycles is practically synonymous with real estate investment. And as usual, everyone remotely connected with the industry – and his dog – has got a well-established theory about where we are in the cycle at any given time. If you talk about the history of cycles, and booms and busts, someone will always try to maintain that 'it won't happen again' – until it happens again. The bad news is that downturns do happen. The good news is that the upswings invariably follow – and that it is never 'too late' to find real opportunities for capital growth.

> Someone will always try to maintain that 'it won't happen again' – until it happens again.

When I was at school, I used to work in my father's menswear shop in country Victoria during the holidays. I'd often start work at 8.30am, and not see a single customer until 11.00am – and then, quite suddenly, four or five unrelated customers would walk in at the same time. You'd expect the same to happen at lunchtime, but then it would be quiet until some random point in the afternoon, when I'd be rushed off my feet all over again.

If you ever wait for trains or buses, you may recognise the same phenomenon. There is no obvious rhyme or reason to the frenzies of activity and inactivity – despite the timetable! In real estate terms, you might expect that falling interest rates would cause increased activity in the residential property market: in fact, the market during the '80s and '90s was never more active than when interest rates were at their highest levels.

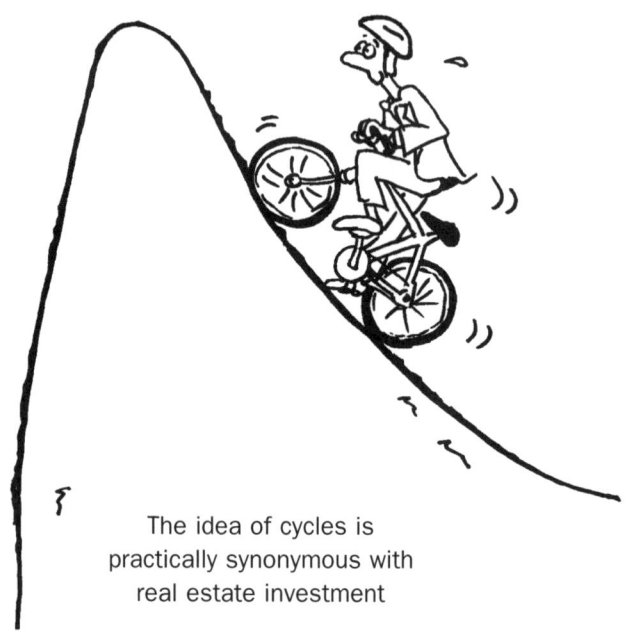

The idea of cycles is practically synonymous with real estate investment

Personally, I don't know where we are in the cycle, and I'm pretty sure that I don't need to know. I think there is a much simpler factor at work behind fluctuations in property values. And that factor is *affordability*.

WHO CONTROLS THE PRICE OF PROPERTY?

The banks and finance companies indirectly control property prices throughout Australia. How? By controlling the amount that they are prepared to lend on residential property.

And what is that decision based on? Affordability: the borrowers' ability to make the necessary loan repayments, as a percentage of their income.

A typical bank lets people pay 30–35% of their disposable income towards mortgage repayments: that's $420 per week of the average household income of $1200 per week. This in turn determines the total amount the bank will lend over the life of the loan.

When the market is booming, and banks go beyond these guidelines, weekly repayments increase to the outer limit of *everybody's* comfort zone – and that's when a crash is looming.

The table on the following page shows mortgage repayments as a percentage of average total monthly earnings since 1991 in the capital cities. In the wake of the 1989–90 recession, mortgage repayments went through the roof, and then everything came crashing down in 1991–92. The dust started to settle in 1993 with repayments reaching a manageable level. You can see that in 2003–08 during the property boom, mortgage repayments were high in comparison to the start of the decade. And what happened post 2008? The GFC, which meant mortgage repayments hit a 10-year low. The rise, fall and settling of repayments means the rise, fall and settling of property prices.

Mortgage repayments as a percentage of average monthly earnings

As at 30 June 2009	Sydney	Melbourne	Brisbane	Adelaide	Perth	Hobart	Canberra	Darwin
1991	33.9	29.2	26.0	24.4	21.1	23.1	18.5	21.4
1992	29.2	24.0	22.6	20.1	18.4	19.4	17.5	19.2
1993	27.4	23.2	21.3	18.9	17.7	20.3	17.0	23.9
1994	27.1	21.6	20.3	17.6	18.3	20.0	15.0	20.5
1995	30.5	22.8	22.2	19.2	20.2	20.6	15.9	24.0
1996	28.2	21.2	20.4	16.8	18.0	20.1	15.3	19.7
1997	24.3	19.7	16.4	13.9	15.4	15.3	12.2	16.5
1998	25.8	21.4	16.2	13.7	15.3	14.9	12.1	16.2
1999	26.8	22.6	16.1	14.1	15.2	15.5	11.2	14.8
2000	32.9	27.3	18.9	16.5	17.2	18.9	14.2	17.2
2001	30.1	26.7	16.9	15.0	16.1	15.2	13.0	15.0
2002	35.7	28.1	18.5	16.1	16.7	15.3	13.9	14.9
2003	40.6	29.3	22.6	20.5	17.8	19.9	18.2	14.9
2004	42.6	29.6	28.9	23.4	20.8	27.3	20.9	18.3
2005	39.5	28.2	28.2	25.2	23.7	26.6	19.2	18.5
2006	38.4	28.0	27.7	25.3	30.6	26.9	19.8	21.4
2007	37.6	30.5	29.9	27.1	33.7	28.9	21.7	23.4
2008	41.4	35.1	36.2	33.8	33.7	31.2	24.5	25.9
Forecasts								
2009	29.6	24.5	25.0	24.1	24.0	23.5	16.9	21.3
2010	27.5	23.0	23.5	22.6	22.3	22.0	15.7	20.1
2011	28.6	24.3	24.6	23.6	22.7	22.4	16.5	20.6
2012	31.5	26.4	26.7	25.8	24.4	24.1	17.9	22.0

Mortgage payments of a 25 year loan equal to 75% of the median house price, at the applicable standard bank variable housing interest rate as at 30 June each year.

Source: A.B. S. REIA, RBA, BIS Shrapnel forecasts

AFFORDABILITY ON YOUR SIDE

I recommend building a portfolio of property at the bottom end of the real estate market: that is, within a band where the property is most affordable.

Monitor the value of properties *in relation to average total weekly earnings:* you can get the statistics from the Australian Bureau of Statistics in the city where you are planning to invest. Establish what you consider an affordable purchase price – around the banks' comfort zone marker of 30–35% – as the *upper limit of what you will pay for an investment property.*

Having an upper limit of 30–35% of average income is consistent with our rental practices as well, since the price of the property will determine the rent we will be able and willing to charge, and we want that to be accessible to 90% of our target market.

Let's see how average property prices compare to our measure of affordability in the capital cities.

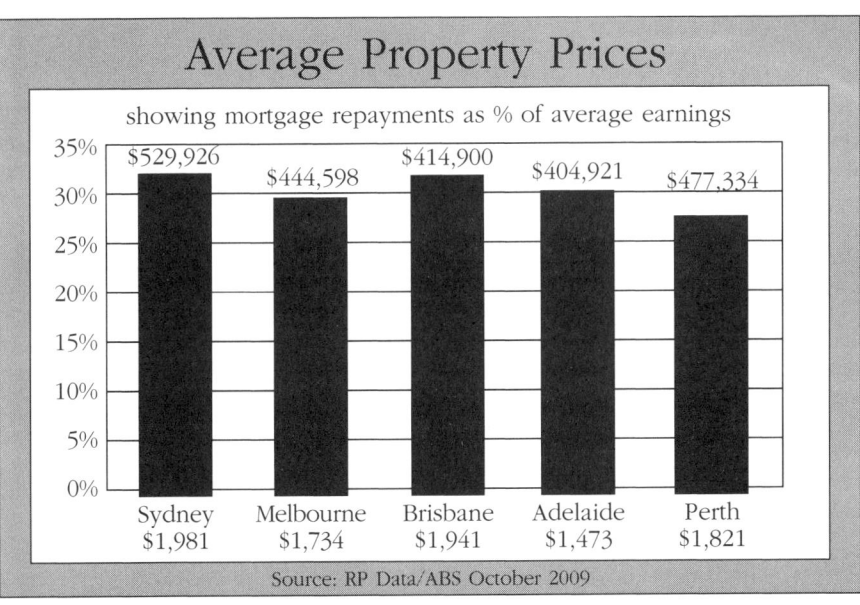

Average Property Prices
showing mortgage repayments as % of average earnings

	Sydney	Melbourne	Brisbane	Adelaide	Perth
Price	$529,926	$444,598	$414,900	$404,921	$477,334
Weekly	$1,981	$1,734	$1,941	$1,473	$1,821

Source: RP Data/ABS October 2009

- Both Brisbane and Sydney currently show good affordability: they could probably go to 33–34% before you would start getting concerned about your ability to duplicate.

- Perth shows up as an undervalued market: there is a lot of room for affordability. The city also has high economic growth prospects and is the home to a number of large infrastructure projects. Mark it down as a growth area to watch.

- Adelaide and Melbourne also have room to move, based on affordability. In fact, Melbourne is definitely a city to watch and invest in with great affordability.

The point is that affordability is linked to average weekly earnings and interest rates. Wages and salaries don't, generally, tend to fall. But you need to keep an eye on interest rates, because if they rise, they can affect the above graph pretty quickly.

In the wake of the GFC, the market is unpredictable. If you study the *national* median house price over the last 30–50 years, though, the only time it has actually fallen was during a World War. And even on a state by state basis, over the last 30 years, the median hasn't fallen off more than 10% during a so-called 'crash'. Generally, house prices may flatten out for five or six years with depressed demand – but if you purchased housing, which is predominantly owned by occupiers, that's the worst of it. And it tends to affect the higher end of the market, rather than the lower end: Sydney and some parts of Melbourne may see that effect in the next few years. Lower-end property still builds value well – but doesn't lose it badly when the cycle turns.

> **Lower-end property still builds value well – but doesn't lose it badly when the cycle turns.**

I find that land generally tends to hold its value pretty well: less so, buildings. It's often purchasers' paying over-inflated prices for buildings that causes the mirage referred to as a 'boom'. In my experience, the fall-off in property prices mainly affects the middle to higher range, where investors have paid huge premiums on buildings – inherently short-lived, replaceable products – in the mistaken perception of an under-supply. This really exposed itself during the GFC in 2008–09 where the top end properties in all capital cities fell by 25–30%.

Over a ten year period, a lot of purchasing mistakes can be recovered and redeemed in housing – but not in units, where you lack the cushion of the land content. You may be sick of my saying it by now, but (one more time): it's the land that offers capital growth; the house is just a vehicle for generating income and tax deductions, in order to offset our outlays on acquiring the land.

THE UPSIDE OF THE BOTTOM END

Affordability cushions the effects of property cycles. It also ensures that, when you decide to sell your investment property (as discussed in the following chapter), you know that anybody with a job will be able to buy it. As you will see from the following table, once a property reaches $500,000 in value, less than 20% of the market can afford to buy it. At about $700,000, your potential buyers are less than 5% of the 'affordable' market.

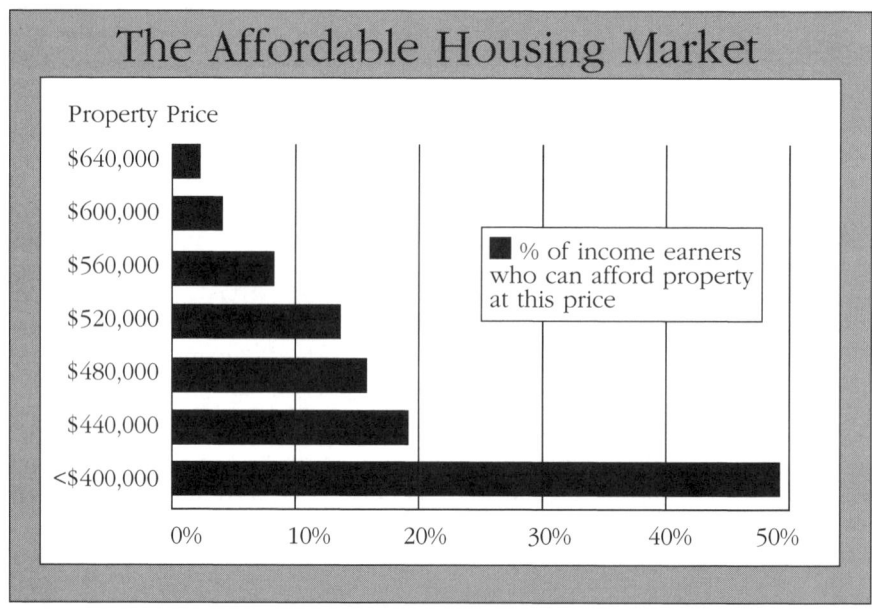

Notes:
1. Based on the average full-time adult weekly income (ABS 2009) of $1338
2. Assuming 25% deposit, P & I loan @ 7%, 30% gross income apportioned to mortgage payments
3. Approximately 45% of the population earn less than $700 per week. They have not been included in the percentages.

So you are better off buying two properties at $400,000 than one property at $800,000. One hundred per cent of the qualified market can afford to rent your properties at the price you can afford to charge, thus ensuring that you optimise your income over time – especially since you have your income eggs in more than one basket, spreading the risk of vacancy or other local glitches. And 100% of the qualified market can afford to buy your properties whenever you wish to liquidate your assets.

Case example

One investor from North Queensland had $50,000 to invest. He was considering putting it into one property of around $300,000, which would have shown him an income of $300 per week – with limited depreciation, negative-gearing potential and capital growth. After one of our seminars, he instead bought three *new* properties for $365,000 (in 1998), borrowing $328,000. The rental income/interest equation left him with no cash outlays, and he got an immediate tax deduction of $18,000 per annum, through depreciation. Most importantly, his properties collectively are now worth well over $800,000.

So, finally, let's look at if, when and how to sell your properties to maximise capital growth.

Notes

Chapter 9 [Step 6]
Make time work for you

Some people trade in the property market – constantly buying and selling – quite successfully.

Actually, when I say 'some' people, I mean perhaps 0.01% of investors.

Buying and selling property is *expensive:* around 12% of the initial purchase price can be thrown away in stamp duty, fees, charges, commission on resale and so on. This is often the forgotten factor when people buy 'fixer uppers'. They add value through renovation and sell on at a higher price – but rarely high enough to offset the costs of renovation *and* the costs of buying and selling!

As you may have noticed, the wealth building concept is a longer-term acquisition plan. It's based on long-term factors (like the historical capital growth of residential house-and-land packages, building equity) and offers long-term benefits. (Sorry, but you don't get rich quick, you just get rich slow).

The key is to buy, and keep buying, and to *hold*. To let **Assets + Time = Wealth.**

TIME WORKS – WHEN YOU DO!

I might have called this chapter 'Time for Discipline'. A lot of people get excited by the growth history of property, and the prospect of building serious wealth – and often, they lack the discipline, patience and commitment to see it through.

Ironically, this is especially true of some of the high-powered executive types who come to our seminars. They are happy to agree with all the principles, but confess that building wealth, the way I have portrayed, simply isn't as exciting as going out and doing a deal and making hundreds of thousands of dollars in one 'hit'.

Fair enough. I've got to admit, myself, that our wealth building structure is not all that exciting. It's not a thrill-a-minute gamble. It asks you to wait and 'watch the grass grow'. But there's also a reasonable expectation that beneath that grass – in the land – lie dollars and capital appreciation!

Or let's go back to our muscle-building analogy of Chapter 3. The muscle only grows when it is being rested. When muscle-builders become over-enthusiastic, or downright impatient, and do not rest sufficiently after carrying out an exercise, they end up breaking down from stress. Unfortunately, this can occur in the financial situation, too: banks, accountants and advisors are the first ones to point out if your business has grown too quickly or too soon, and to advise you to put the brakes on.

> **Our wealth building structure is not all that exciting.**

'Making time work for you' is really about establishing the discipline and commitment to acquire six properties over a ten year period, building on the history of the last 90 years, to plan for a 8% per annum capital growth factor.

(If that's *really* too 'slow' for you, you might want to check out my Accelerated Wealth program called *Untold Wealth*. But remember the story of the tortoise and the hare: slow and steady really can get over that finish line – if not first, at least with less stress.)

Let's look again at the basic financial goal for duplication which we introduced in Chapter 3, before all our principles were in place.

Here's where you can end up if you start today, purchasing a property, of the kind we've been talking about, in the way we've been talking about, at $500,000.

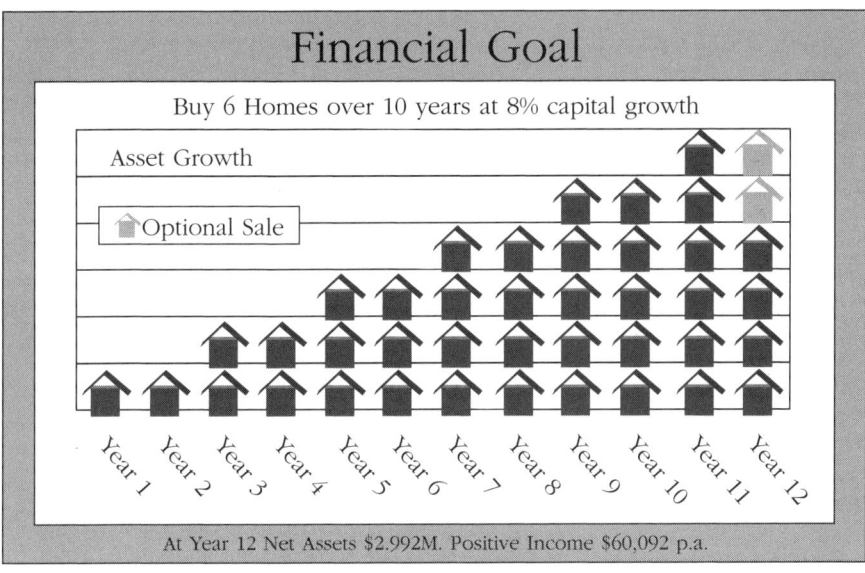

OK. ARE YOU SITTING DOWN?

If you acquire these properties over a ten year period:
- you will have paid $3,226,931 for your portfolio; and
- you will have a debt of $3,226,931 (if you do not pay off any principal).

Just let that sink in for a moment. It may sound scary. But remember:
- you will also have sufficient *income* to service that entire debt – *and* many of your other outlays (based on interest rates at 7%).

And here are some more reassuring – perhaps even exciting – numbers.
- In Year 10, your property portfolio will be worth around $4.7 million growing by nearly $384,000 per annum.

- In Year 12, you'll have *net* assets of around $2.44 million *still growing,* at that stage by nearly $414,500 per annum (and rising).

If that doesn't make you feel any happier, let's put those debt numbers into perspective.

- If you started building your six-property portfolio around *1965,* it would have a value today of over *$2.4 million.* And even if you had borrowed 100% and never paid a cent of principal, you would have debt of less than *$140,000.*
- If you started building your six-property portfolio around *1975,* the value of your properties would be over *$2.5 million* today, and – without your repaying any of the principal – your debt would be around *$350,000.*
- If you started building your six-property portfolio in *1985,* you would still have value of over *$3 million* today, with a debt (without having repaid principal) of just *$1 million.*

And you'd also have the rental *income* from the six properties, which would easily service a principal and interest loan *and* give you some income *and* you'd have capital growth of over $100,000 a year, which would *compound* over the next 10 years.

These debts that you might have been carrying from the '60s, '70s or '80s don't seem so scary when you think where you've got to. This may be a helpful perspective for starting your wealth building. $1.8 million (in ten years) may seem a lot of debt to carry, but:

- it is being reliably serviced – without drawing too heavily on your personal cash flow or other resources

- at that stage, your equity is growing by $250,000–300,000 per annum.

People often challenge me with the assertion that, since inflation is low, property won't grow at the same rate. Indeed, I read all sorts of 'expert' opinions preaching this as some new financial gospel. Where do they get it from? If you stayed awake to the property markets around Australia, for example, during 1997–2000, you'd be aware that property tends to rebound to make up for limited capital growth in slower years. We need to look coolly at the effects of inflation. During the '60s, we had an average inflation of approximately 2.5% – and property prices in some capital cities grew at a massive 13% per annum.

My personal opinion is that inflation really just props up building costs, and therefore *units,* which have a high building content. And, throughout the '60s, '70s and '80s, the growth in *house* values, as a percentage, has outperformed units and townhouses.

HOW DO YOU MAKE TIME WORK FOR YOU?

From a long-term perspective, there need be no barriers to wealth building. It merely requires a disciplined commitment in two areas:

1. *Keep buying* over the ten year period (unless the principle of affordability has been made impossible by a greedy phase of the market in a particular area).
2. *Take one step at a time.*

We'll look at each of these commitments in turn.

KEEP BUYING

With an average property growth of 8% over the 10 year period, you will have six opportunities to use your increased equity to acquire further property. You might be 'sitting out' of the market for perhaps three years out of the ten.

The time to sit out of the market is when the factors in property pricing (indirectly controlled, as we noted, by the lending institutions) are out of step with average income, and therefore beyond the level of general affordability in a particular area.

Remember our table of mortgage repayments as a percentage of average weekly earnings (in Chapter 8)?

Things went crazy in 1989 and 1990 in Sydney and Melbourne, as repayments went to 60–78% of the average earnings.

House prices crashed in 1991, before settling down in 1992 and 1993. If we were building our portfolio at this time, monitoring the market according to our principle of affordability, we would have sat out of the market in Sydney and Melbourne from 1988 right through to 1991. We could have come back in 1992, perhaps even picking up prime opportunities because of the desperation of a panicked market, in which the banks are selling up less careful investors. This is called *counter-cyclical buying*. The moral is: don't be a herd investor. Don't buy when everybody else does, when property begins to rise. Buy when everyone else is selling, and sell when everyone else is buying. Better yet: never sell!

Sydney and Melbourne seem particularly vulnerable to boom-time problems, perhaps because of the density and size of their population, and the confidence that the banks derive from having their head offices located in those cities, where they deal with major corporate players. Notice that in Brisbane, Adelaide and Perth, there was nowhere near the same frenzy of mortgage repayments out of kilter with affordability.

You might have chosen to sit out of the market in Brisbane during 1989–90 – but even if you bought during those times, your capital appreciation still would have shown some growth in 1991–93.

Don't be a herd investor

In any case, if you use your affordability principles, you can judge when to wait and when to buy again, without over-reaching yourself or slowing your capital growth. And in order to accelerate and maintain your portfolio development, remember: *you do need to keep buying.*

As we noted in Chapter 7, less than 1.5% of all individual investors acquire more than four properties. With a bit of discipline and commitment to keep buying, you're putting yourself among the very top wealth builders.

> Acquiring six properties over a ten year period – and holding onto them as a retirement plan – WORKS.

ONE STEP AT A TIME

Acquiring six properties over a ten year period – and holding onto them as a retirement plan – WORKS.

Of course, you could accelerate or slow down this process, to suit your own capacity and confidence.

The important point is to take each step at a time.

Don't be mesmerised at this stage by the thought of owing $3 million, or having to manage six properties. Like climbing a mountain, it may look a long way from the bottom to the top, but you get there one step at a time: one property at a time. Give yourself a year or two to settle in, to work out some of the kinks, to establish your structure firmly, so that there really is no drain on your resources. Let your confidence build with each successful step. And then, when the fresh equity is there, think about purchasing again.

Some people say to me that they just *can't* come to grips with the idea of that amount of debt, or owning six properties: they think, because they can't see themselves, as they are today, going from *here* to *there,* all of a sudden, that it's just not for them. That's like letting the mountain conquer you before you have even taken a step. The thing to remember is that:

> Like climbing a mountain, it may look a long way from the bottom to the top, but you get there one step at a time.

- you don't have to do it all at once – just one step at a time
- you don't have to do the whole journey with the resources or the perspective that you start with: the journey itself equips you as you go forward.

'Making time work for you' means trusting that all your resources (equity, knowledge, experience, perspective) will grow and mature as the journey proceeds. You have enough to *start* with. And, with this structure, *you are in control.* At each step – as at the 'end' of the journey – there are *options,* depending on what you want to achieve and what the market is doing.

Let's look at some of the most attractive of those options.

OPTION 1: CONVERT YOUR LOAN TO PRINCIPAL & INTEREST, AFTER 5 YEARS

I personally like the strategy of converting the investment loan on a property to principal & interest, after you have owned that property for five years. Rental income growth of between 3% and 4% per annum should allow you to convert your interest-only loan to P & I in Year 6 or 7 – and *still* maintain a minimal cash outlay.

Over time, the tenant will then be paying off your mortgage.

You should be aware that the principal is not tax deductible, so you may, following conversion of the loan, have to pay tax. You should also be aware that in the first five years of a 20-year P & I loan, you only pay off between 12% and 15% of the total principal: it is in the last five years that you really see the compound effect of your principal repayments. However, this is a step in the right direction, and can give you some peace of mind, if you're looking to pay off the principal on multiple properties and hold onto them (as they keep generating income) as a retirement plan and/or to pass on to your kids.

OPTION 2: SELL, AND REPAY YOUR DEBT

Selling one or more of your properties is, of course, an option, in order to reduce some or all of the debt on the rest of your portfolio. You need to think about:
- what to sell and
- when to sell.

Selling is particularly attractive in a boom time, when the market may be more optimistic than realistic.

The best time to sell is when everyone else is buying. And that includes that typical two-year peak in the 'cycle' when affordability parameters seem to have gone out the window! You could see the value of your portfolio increase by 25–30% *above* its 'true' value for a two-year period (before coming down). Some investors – and a lot of speculators – try and take advantage of this cyclical movement, which we've learned to identify.

So what happens, if you take advantage of the cyclical peak?

Well, if you sold your *last* two properties (acquired in Years 8 and 10, with the cycle working in your favour), and you sold them in Year 12 at the peak of the market, instead of an average 30% increase, you might have a 50% increase on your purchase price. So, if the properties cost you $1.3 million and are now worth $1.6 million, you may have an opportunity to sell them for $1.9 million: a profit of $600,000 instead of $300,000.

Capital Gains Tax for individuals

When you sell (or otherwise dispose of) an asset acquired after 19 September 1985, you are liable for Capital Gains Tax (CGT) on any increased value, or profit. In terms of property, your *home* is exempt: investment property, unfortunately, isn't. Highly simplified, the amount of taxable capital gain is calculated as the sale price (consideration) *minus* the acquisition cost of the property, adjusted by the depreciation claimed on it, and reduced by 50% where the property has been held for a period of 12 months or more.

In our example, CGT is worked out on the $290,000 profit discounted by 50%. So if you held those last two properties for two years and three years respectively, the calculation would work as follows.

	Property 5 (Year 9)	Property 6 (Year 10)	Total (Year 12)
Purchase price	$635,000	$700,000	$1,335,000
Building Allowance	$8,000	$9,000	$17,000
Sale Price	$820,000	$820,000	$1,690,000
Book Profit	$185,000	$120,000	$305,000
Less			
Capital Gain	$177,000	$111,000	$288,000
50% discount	$88,500	$55,500	$144,000
Equals			
Taxable Profit (gain)	$88,500	$55,500	$144,000

You would have to pay CGT on a total of $144,000 (after twelve years of investment). This would amount to $67,680 – based on the *highest* marginal rate of income tax.

Three points to note:

1. The above calculation applies to all property purchased by individuals after 21 September 1999 (when the CGT rules changed) which is held for 12 months prior to sale. If a property is held for less than 12 months, you must pay tax on the total book profit.

2. Where a property was purchased prior to 21 September 1999, you have the option of calculating the amount of your taxable gain using the above discount method or you may choose to calculate the taxable gain as the sale price (consideration received) *minus* the acquisition cost of the property, indexed for inflation to 30 September 1999. (Don't panic.

Tax is simply a factor of doing business.

Most people don't do their own CGT calculations: they keep their basic purchase/ expenditure/sale records and hand them over to a competent accountant. Highly recommended.)

3. If you've sold during a boom, the property may well have been inflated above its true value by almost the total amount of tax you have to pay! So waiting for the boom glitch in the cycle, and taking that opportunity to sell, is a way of minimising the impact of CGT.

Goods and Services Tax

Since the introduction of a Goods and Services Tax (GST) on 1 July 2000, it is necessary to consider its impact on the sale of the property. Before a sale can be subject to GST, however, you must be registered for GST. You only need to become registered when your annual turnover exceeds $75,000 per annum *excluding* rental income and salary and wages income.

The short version of the story is that unless you are in the business of buying and selling newly constructed properties on a regular basis (buying or selling more than one new property every 12 months) you should not need to register for GST. If you do not need to register then you do not need to include GST in the price for which you sell the property. (This position will be different if you are conducting a business in your name.) Again this should be clarified with a competent accountant.

Tax is simply a factor of doing business. It's one of the reasons why you might consider *not* selling, but *holding* your properties as they keep generating income over time. If you decide to sell, you need to be aware that CGT is a factor. If you are selling on a regular basis (which is not recommended) then GST may be a factor.

OPTION 3: REDEVELOP THE PROPERTIES WITH A HIGHER-DENSITY ZONING

As we have noted, the population in Australia's major cities is steadily growing.

The solution developed by town planners over the last few years is *urban infill:* that is, the redevelopment of 600 and 700 square metre blocks to accommodate two, three or four dwellings instead of one. This may be an option for you in 20–30 years' time, if you are still holding a portfolio (as I recommend). Remember, it's the *land* that's of value.

You won't be able to take advantage of higher density building if you own a town house, or if you share the land with another landlord in a group title, but owning a house does give you this flexibility. In Melbourne, Sydney and Brisbane, they have already allowed dual occupancy, and it won't be long (say, 10–20 years) before they allow higher density again, on these smaller lots. This may effectively give you the opportunity, with your equity, to build 3–4 income-generating properties on your allotment. I'd still encourage you not to sell them, but to keep the land for further growth.

This has been the secret of a lot of car yards, which bought fringe CBD sites on main roads, 10–20 years ago, and now find those sites commanding a premium and being re-developed as fast food restaurants, shopping centres and so on. Even if their businesses have only broken even, these car dealers are very wealthy individuals today, because they owned and held onto the land.

SUMMARY

The benefits of letting time work for you are enormous: just glance back at the financial goal graph on page 139.

Perhaps the most important thing I've said in this chapter, though, is this: TAKE ONE STEP AT A TIME.

If we look too far ahead, before we're confident with where we are and where the next step is, we can scare ourselves with all kinds of mirages of things that might go wrong, that we might not know how to deal with (yet). The thing about mirages is, when you actually get there, they tend to disappear. But confidence is a major part of successful – not stressful – wealth building.

So in Part C, I deal with some of the 'What if?' and 'What about?' questions that you might still have. I get those questions all the time. And it's great – it's vital – that they get asked. When you're about to start a journey, it's natural to look for potholes in the road. As I said, right at the start, sceptics make the best wealth builders. But the fact is, no-one's got a crystal ball. There's no such thing as having 'all the answers' (or even 'all the questions') ahead of time. Sooner or later, you've got to choose to take a first step – and that's when the real answers start coming.

You've just had eight chapters of data, pros and cons, principles and options and suggestions. I'm glad if you feel better informed now than when you started this book. But I'd also like you to keep sight of our starting point: the sense of a journey, and the new possibilities that open up as you dare to think about creating wealth, for yourself and others.

So in Chapter 10, let's look, one more time, at where we're headed.

GLOBAL FINANCIAL CRISIS

It has been interesting to looking back over the past 10 years at housing affordability in Australia. The residential markets have had a tremendous run in price growth in 1997, 1998 and 2003 on the east coast. My clients and I were principally buying in Brisbane and to a lesser extent in Melbourne during those times.

In 2003, the markets on the east coast peaked, as did affordability. However, it created an opportunity to by on the west coast in Perth. While property on the east coast was selling for mid $300,000 in 2004–05, we were buying property in Perth in the $200,000 range in 2003–2005. The market in Perth significantly increased in value. By 2006, everything we purchased in 2003–05 increased to around $500,000. As we moved back to the east coast, we were able to continue buying in and around Brisbane and Melbourne in the $300,000 market in good locations.

All those prices sub $300,000 look very affordable even during the GFC.

Notes

Notes

Chapter 10 *[Step 7]*
Be all you can be

Early on in this book, I hoped to plant a seed in your mind that, as you begin to build wealth, you may find yourself getting back more than you expected: more than financial rewards. I shared with you my own belief that everything has a purpose – and that, through building wealth, I began to discover mine. I'd always felt I had potential – but for what? I started out with the goal of being wealthy, and it was as I reached that goal that I found the goal posts had moved forever.

How do you feel about the idea of being wealthy? Powerful? Excited? Quietly secure: it's just a way to meet your day-to-day needs and those of your family? Or perhaps a little bit guilty or embarrassed? (Some people do.) What possibilities are you allowing yourself to look forward to? And are they really the best you can expect *for* yourself – and *of* yourself?

One of the qualities shared by wealthy people is that they are pro-active: they see opportunities, and make things happen. You might have glimpsed an opportunity as you read this book. You might even go out and make it happen. And being pro-active tends to make you *more* pro-active, because when you're out there, you begin to notice things that you may not have noticed before, and to have the confidence to do something about them. This kind of mental preparedness may be part of your potential: think how useful it could be in all sorts of areas of your life.

THE BIG PICTURE ON WEALTH

Something like 0.0001% of the world's population controls 99% of the world's wealth.

Apparently, a computer model has demonstrated that if all that wealth was distributed equally amongst every living person, within about 15 years it would have filtered back to the 0.0001%. Whether this is true or not, isn't it an amazing concept? What it means to me is that those few of us who are fortunate and knowledgeable enough to create, control and enjoy wealth have a responsibility towards those who aren't and don't. We are not just wealthy individuals: we are custodians of the world's wealth in our society.

> **We are not just wealthy individuals: we are custodians of the world's wealth in our society.**

And that means that if you are in the wealth building business, you have a purpose and a responsibility *wider* than meeting your own needs and the needs of your family.

'ALL THAT MAN IS, IS INFINITE. ALL THAT MAN HAS, IS FINITE.'

Some people talk as if 'you can't take it with you' is a negative thing, and a reason not to bother creating wealth at all. Personally, I find it an energising and empowering idea. I can't take my wealth with me: therefore, I'll both *enjoy* it – and *pass it on*. While I'm alive, I'm 'minding' a portion of the world's wealth, and I can 'pass it on' in all sorts of ways: in improved living conditions and opportunities for others now, and in self-sustaining capital and wealth-preserving knowledge for the future.

There comes a time in your wealth building journey when you realise that you have 'enough' wealth to be able to retire. It became clear to me in 1990 that I was getting close: by 1991, I could have retired with an annual income of $300,000 for the rest of my life. It was what I'd always thought I wanted, but when I got there, retiring on my wealth seemed like a huge cop-out. I still needed a challenge and a purpose. At the same time, I couldn't see making *more* (and more) money, for the sake of it, as very fulfilling or purposeful. And that's when the 'custodian' perspective kicked in, for me.

My wife and I decided to establish our own charitable foundation for homeless youth, the plight of whom had concerned us for some time. As 'luck' (or whatever) would have it, we met husband and wife psychologists Dr Ron and Suwanti Farmer, and together, we established the Toogoolawa Children's Home. We started out in Sydney, providing full-time residential care to youth at risk (generally Wards of the State) who had been psychologically damaged within their families.

TOOGOOLAWA: A PLACE IN THE HEART

The Toogoolawa Children's Home

'Toogoolawa' is an aboriginal word meaning 'a place in the heart': our belief is that, whatever physical abuse children have suffered, there is a place within themselves where they can find healing and strength and meaning.

Toogoolawa has now fostered over 500 young people – with tremendous success, given that some of them (as young as 11 and 12-years-old) had been in anything up to 18 other foster homes before coming to Toogoolawa: many of the kids stay with us until they are 15 or 16 years old and ready to live independently.

In 1993, we moved the home to Brisbane, and since then have expanded Toogoolawa to include a school and community service (initiated by the young people themselves). We now have a residential care program offering:

- long-term placement for 12–15 year olds
- emergency placement (for periods not longer than 7 days) for 12–15 year olds
- planned respite placement (for periods not longer than 2 weeks) for 12–15 year olds living at home or in other care
- a Shared Family Care Program, offering long- and short-term placement in caring homes. We recruit, train and supervise foster parents for up to 12 troubled teenagers.

The Toogoolawa Schools

The first school was established in 1998 on the Pimpama Rivers Estate I developed at Ormeau in South East Queensland. It offers education and opportunity to kids who have been expelled from, are no longer welcome in, or do not feel fulfilled by, mainstream schooling. When we began to research the need, we were alarmed to find that every year there were up to 300 children aged under 15, in the Brisbane area alone, who had been expelled from the public school system, and weren't attending school.

I don't blame the public school system: these kids are, quite often, 'difficult' and disruptive in a 'normal' classroom environment. But it is their right – and our responsibility – to see they get some type of education. (This is another area where 'expert' opinions and statistics are rampant, and I'm not going to labour the point. But it may interest you to learn that, of the prison population in Australia, 95% are from broken families and over 60% are illiterate. Perhaps, if we start with change in these areas, as a community, we can begin to turn around the social decay that we are all so aware of and so frequently daunted by. Like wealth building: start small, and think big. Radical change happens one step at a time.)

> Radical change happens one step at a time.

The Toogoolawa School offers a basic education and a simple, positive philosophy to live by: that service, truthfulness and consideration for others leads to a happy, fulfilled and effective life. The students are taught not only to read, write and spell, but to speak and listen and calculate – and to strive to discern right from wrong, and to see the value in following the former.

The Toogoolawa School at Ormeau also operates as a mobile unit, utilising the ideal learning environment of the outdoors. By combining fun and physical activity with experiential learning techniques, students begin to see learning as immediate and relevant, and develop a sense of responsibility for their choices and actions.

The five universal human values of love, truth, peace, right conduct and non-violence are integrated into all aspects of the school curriculum. The teachers endeavour to become role models for these values, and convey to the students that these qualities already lie within each one of them, like a diamond hidden inside a mountain.

Regular sharing sessions help to develop communication skills – and a sense of community is important too: students regularly visit a nursing home for the elderly, and assist at a work facility (SWARA) for the developmentally disabled, as part of our commitment to community service. We strive for a balance between *support* (with an emphasis on social interaction and exploration of spirituality and ecology) and *challenge*, in order to empower and inspire our students to acknowledge and achieve their potential.

Buoyed with our success in 'educare' (learning how to care) in Queensland, we opened another Toogoolawa School in Newcastle (NSW) in 2002 and one in Hastings (Victoria) in 2005. The schools are funded in large part by a small group of Custodian WealthBuilders. Further schools are planned, with a long term goal of 20. Start small: think big.

THE SMALL DIFFERENCE
THAT MAKES A BIG DIFFERENCE

The most common excuse for doing nothing is also the most simple: someone else will do it.

In 1994, I was at a dinner sponsored by the Committee for Economic Development of Australia (CEDA), with 12 top business people from major public companies. In hindsight, I'm not actually sure how I fitted into this group, but it was certainly an eye-opener for all of us. I was asked to talk about my work with Toogoolawa over the preceding four years, and particularly, about (a) the costs of operating such a charity and (b) how you would measure its performance or 'success'.

I explained that the cost of full-time care and schooling, in the intensive environment we have created, can range from $30,000–50,000 per child, per annum. I distinctly recall the comment of one flabbergasted diner, to the effect that such a cost was simply unjustifiable, and that I was wasting my money. Some of the other business people present felt that it was the government's obligation – already sufficiently supported by our taxes – to cater for such needs.

What are we made of?

If you were walking down the street, and you saw, on the other side, an eight-year-old child lying bleeding and crying on the pavement, would you cross the road to help?

Chapter 10 - Be all you can be | 161

Of course, there would be plenty of excuses *not* to go... Too busy; late for an appointment (*would* have gone, naturally, but the appointment was very important); new suit, didn't want to get blood on it; the child's out of danger now; anyway, things don't look *that* bad – from where you're standing... The most common excuse for doing nothing is also the most simple: someone else will do it.

And this is exactly what's happening, in effect, in our society, every day. When our psychologist started looking into the incidence of child abuse, we were horrified at the numbers we uncovered – and those were only the cases that had come to the attention of the authorities. If our children are a reflection of how we are handling our responsibility and moral custodianship, we need to wake up and get our act together – fast.

At Toogoolawa, we've seen kids who, by the time they are 11–12 years old, have been in 15 foster homes and a dozen schools. After the damage they've sustained – in the supposed 'sanctuary' of their own homes – they don't trust anyone. Their distress bursts out in anger and aggression. And so it begins: they go from home to home and from school to school, setting themselves up for rejection after rejection: the only pattern they've ever known.

But at Toogoolawa, we've seen the vicious circle broken. Some of the kids spend the rest of their adolescence with us. Which means that we can begin to help them work through some of their problems. We can give them time to discover that what has happened to them isn't the best they can expect from other people. And that there is some goodness, after all, in the world – and within themselves. Hence the name Toogoolawa: a place in the heart.

Like wealth building, it's a long-term program: no quick fixes. When kids first come to us, they are – understandably – pretty angry. Three years later, you can see the anger being channelled into something more positive and supportive for them. They have begun to develop some self esteem, to feel good about themselves, perhaps for the first time in their lives.

> If this is the kind of thing you'd like to get involved in, let me encourage you: it needn't be too far away.

SOWING THE SEED

As you can probably tell, I'm pretty committed to – and excited by – my work with the Toogoolawa project. For the last 12 years, I have committed over $300,000 a year to it. And the fact is, it's been *enriching:* perhaps the most fulfilling thing I've done in my life.

I started out only providing the money to run the program, and assist with the administration: we have a great team of psychologists and social workers who work hands-on with the kids and are a constant inspiration to me and to others who come to take a look at the Toogoolawa effect in action. But I was soon challenged to give something more of myself: running outdoor education and effective communication classes, allowing me to share another passion I have, for hiking, with the kids.

It's making a small difference that makes a big difference.

We all share the responsibility to maintain humanity and justice and opportunity in our society. My hope is that other businesses could take responsibility – and find purpose – in funding similar programs: they have the resources and administrative capabilities that welfare agencies often lack.

As for you, if this is the kind of thing you'd like to get involved in, let me encourage you: it needn't be too far away. Once you have a portfolio of four or five homes, you could use the equity to purchase perhaps an older home, which you could dedicate to people in need.

Why an older home? Well, it depends what you are going to use it for, but we had one great kid at Toogoolawa who used to have a monthly fit of rage and frustration – and put his fist through the wall. (He was with us for three years, and by the end, those rages were down to one every six months. He was responsible for repairing and repainting the wall himself – and he got quite good at it. It was amazing to see the pride he took in patching and painting the plaster, and decorating his room so that the damage – like the anger – didn't have to be a daily part of his life.)

The acquisition may be structured so that the interest can be claimed as a negatively-geared tax deduction, and you could still get the benefit of capital growth, despite the building's age.

Alternatively, if you'd just like to know more about the Toogoolawa Children's Project and others like it, you might want to read my book *We Can Be Heroes*: the extraordinary stories of some 'ordinary' Australians who make a real difference in the world – one step at a time, if that's what it takes. Or just call us and ask about what we do: we'd love to hear from you. You'll find contact details at the back of this book.

The small difference that makes a big difference...

I'd like to tell you a story, told to me by Dr Ron Farmer.

An old man went down to the beach in the morning, where the surf roared onto the still cool sand at the lowest of the tide. And the beach was covered with starfish, stranded by the tide, as far as the eye could see. And the old man bent and began picking up the starfish and throwing them, one by one, back into the water.

A young runner in a grey tracksuit passed, and stopped, and turned and said: 'What are you doing? Can't you see that you're wasting your time? There are hundreds of starfish here. Your throwing a few back won't make a bit of difference.'

The old man simply bent, and picked up another rough shape in his rough hand, and threw the starfish out into the water with a quiet splash. And said: 'It made a difference to that one.'

Finding a wider, deeper purpose for your wealth building can enrich you on many levels. It can provide the fire and commitment you need to keep going, to start small and think big: it can positively contribute to your success in building wealth. More importantly, perhaps, it can stretch what you may have seen as the limits of your potential, and what it means to be all you can be.

Chapter 10 - Be all you can be

Notes

PART C
Any other questions?

Chapter 11
What about...?

This is the chapter where I promised to answer some of the 'Yes But...' and 'What if...?' questions that people often bring to our seminars. I don't want to put doubts in your mind, where none may have existed, but you may find this chapter helpful for added confidence – or perhaps as a prompt to other questions you'll want to ask as you investigate the wealth building concept further.

I have arranged the queries in alphabetical order by topic, so you can use this as a quick reference tool, as things occur to you.

GOODS AND SERVICES TAX

Q: If I acquire properties and rent them out for residential use, do I need to collect GST?

A: Without getting too technical, from a GST perspective residential rent is input taxed. This essentially means that a residential landlord is not required to collect GST on residential rent.

The residential landlord will, however, *pay* GST when incurring expenses associated with the property such as repairs and maintenance and agent's fees. The residential landlord will not be able to claim a GST input tax credit for the GST included in these expenses. The total amount of the expense, however, including the amount of GST, will be allowed as an income tax deduction.

While this may increase the landlord's operating expenses, it is anticipated that rents will gradually increase to take account of the flow-through effect of GST.

The good news is that GST should have a positive impact on the value of property in Australia.

ECONOMIC CYCLES

Q: What if property doesn't go up by as much as it has done in the past – or even falls in value?
A: See Chapter 8.

INABILITY TO FIND A TENANT

Q: What if I can't get a tenant for my property?
A: See Chapter 5, and 'Loss of tenant', on page 172.

INTEREST RATES

Q: What if interest rates increase?
A: The good news is that when interest rates increase, it means that the economy is moving, and your property is going up in value, and so are rents. The bad news is: your costs are increasing too.

One solution is to lock in your loans: all of them, or a percentage of your portfolio, at any time. Establish with your bank, when you begin your wealth building program, that you'd like to have the flexibility to lock in a rate at any time, or a percentage of your total portfolio loan, given that you may float some as variable and some as fixed. The fixed rate for five years is generally around 1% more than the variable rate. (This may seem a small amount, but you should be looking at each percentage point as costing you $60–70 per week in cash going out of your pocket – so you need to watch it very, very closely.)

Don't be greedy. If you are comfortable with your repayments, as they are now, why not lock in?

LOAN PROBLEMS

Q: What if the bank won't lend me the money for a further property on the equity I've got?

A: Basically, you can either wait – or change banks. Find one which will accept the equity position you want. Make sure you clearly flag your intentions to build a portfolio on this basis. (See Chapter 7.) Don't be surprised if you have to change banks two or three times in your wealth building journey. Banks are often more aggressive about winning new business than about keeping existing clients.

LOSS OF EMPLOYMENT

Q: What if I lose my job?

A: People on PAYG Income Tax Withholding are often concerned that they may lose their job, and – having built up a portfolio of two, three or four properties – may have to sell in the midst of a down cycle (or worse) while simultaneously losing the income advantages of varying the amount of their PAYG Income Tax Withholding.

OK. Put like that, it sounds pretty bad. But you can *insure* against losing your job, if it is a realistic concern in your circumstances or area of employment. You might choose to investigate this insurance. However, the simpler option is to 'self insure', by simply slowing down your wealth building program.

It's not a race to acquire six properties. If it takes eight, ten or twelve years, it's not going to make a great deal of difference in the long run. For peace of mind, if you have a job that you feel is not 100% secure, just be a little less aggressive in your expansion program, for the time being. You may want to have a bit more equity in one property before you acquire the next. Perhaps, rather than starting at 10% equity, start at 20–25%. This is not a reason to do *nothing!*

There may be another option. As an employer, I invite my staff to let me know if they are thinking of acquiring an investment property, so that I can give them honest, forward-looking information about their job. Might your employer be amenable to such a discussion?

LOSS OF TENANT

Q: What if my tenants leave suddenly – or damage the property?

A: It's inevitable that you are going to lose a tenant or two over a 10–12 year period. And if you do lose a tenant, it might take you a couple of weeks to clean the place up and find another one. This is just a factor of the rental income business. Get used to the idea – and plan accordingly.

I forecast my income based on 48-49 weeks' rent per year. I also keep a two-week contingency fund in the account for each property – just for incidentals (or 'accidentals').

You can have some assurance. Get a bond from all tenants of at least one month's rent, and require that they pay their rent in advance: preferably monthly, but at least fortnightly. If they're late with their rent, the agent should be on alert to advise you within one or two days, so that arrangements can be made with the tenant, or – if they are having longer-term financial difficulties – so that notices can be given and the property can be inspected. If tenants wish, they can evade paying rent for up to six weeks, so you might lose up to two week's rent. This is insurable, however.

Assuming that tenants have done *everything* in the Nightmare Tenants' Handbook, they could leave you with a few thousand dollars worth of damage that has to be repaired. *Still* not a reason to panic: this is also insurable, except for your excess, which you can limit to $250. The important thing is, don't wait for the claim: get in and clean the property up as soon as the tenant is evicted. Make sure you get quotes and send them to the insurance company – and *get on with getting your property rented again,* as soon as possible.

In my experience, it comes down to financial management and having that little bit in reserve, tucked away for a rainy day. Losing a bad tenant may seem, for a while, like that rainy day, but (a) it is *not* personal – it happens to all of us; and (b) to be honest, 'good riddance'! It's *not* a good reason to wash your hands of a residential portfolio – or the wealth that comes with it!

TAX LAW CHANGES

Q: What if the government abolishes negative gearing?

A: In July 1985, the Federal Labor government disallowed the tax benefits of negative gearing. All losses that were generated had to be rolled up into the cost of the property and deducted, at the time the property was sold, from the Capital Gains Tax. Panic!

Well, actually, no. The change to the accounting process wasn't too disastrous for investors at the time, because it *wasn't retrospective:* anyone who owned negatively geared properties prior to 1985 could continue claiming the deductions. More importantly, however, the change in policy caused a *major* stall in investment in the new residential property market. Suddenly, there was a looming (drastic) shortage in the supply of residential housing for a growing rental population, and an economy-dragging downturn in building activity.

The Treasurer was forced to *reintroduce* negative gearing in September 1987. Any residential property investor who purchased properties during the two-year abolition period was allowed to offset their two-year losses against their assessable income for 1987–88. (*Nice* U-turn.)

Negative gearing hit the political agenda again, with the revelation that people had been using the provisions to purchase *shares:* the government was considering re-abolishing negative gearing to close the loophole. But in 1997, the then Prime Minister, John Howard, made a statement that: 'Negative gearing would not be abolished on residential property.'

Of course, all we can do is work on the knowledge available to us now, and that is:

- you *can* legitimately negatively gear property

- the government is unlikely to abolish negative gearing on residential property in the future because of the proven knock-on effects on housing supply and economic activity

- if the government *did* abolish again, it probably wouldn't be done retrospectively, so any purchase that you made today should be within the safety net of today's taxation laws.

With the introduction of the GST and other taxation reform measures, the Government has not taken the opportunity to review negative gearing. The Commissioner of Taxation, however, has released several rulings in an attempt to restrict split loans, redraw facilities and capitalisation of interest expense. Investors may be prevented from borrowing 150–200% of the property's value over a period of time and negatively gearing on that amount. This would not, in fact, affect our wealth building structure at all.

MANAGEMENT HASSLES

Q: Isn't managing one rental property – let alone a whole portfolio – a major hassle?

A: Not necessarily – and *not* if you get someone else to do it for you!

The choice of agent to manage your property is one of the most important you'll make. Often, would-be landlords fall into the trap of going with the agent who offers them the highest rent: this is not necessarily an indicator of ability to manage a property successfully.

The questions to ask of a prospective agent are the same you'd ask of prospective employees. Whom have they worked for before? What references have they got?

In essence, look for agents who (a) have experience in managing a large rent roll; (b) have limited vacancies for any given period of time, and (c) have managed on behalf of landlords for an extensive period of time.

Don't be shy about asking for over half a dozen references (or more!) and make sure you ring them *all*. Include a reference from at least one landlord whose property is vacant at the time: such clients will often give you a clear insight into any agent you are looking to appoint.

The other important point to determine is exactly what the agent is going to do for you, and how much it is going to cost you. Generally, the agent's job will fall into the following categories.

- Furnishing you with a fully-itemised monthly statement.

- Conducting full internal and external inspections prior to letting – and every three months, along with photographs of the property and a written report.

- Providing direct payment of rent received (within three days of the new month) into the bank account of your choice, or by cheque posted directly to you.
- Lodging all bonds with the Bond Board, paying accounts (with your permission and on your behalf) and attending to all leases and notices pertaining to the property.
- Liaising with all trades people and inspecting all work prior to payment.
- Attending to final inspection on your behalf, prior to the expiry of your 3-month new home maintenance warranty.
- Checking all potential tenants' references, prior to consulting with you on their acceptability.

Most competent agents will do all of the above for you, and will include it in their management fee.

VALUATIONS

Q: What if the bank refuses to disclose its valuation?

A: This is a *must-have* piece of information. The simple answer is: if one bank won't disclose the valuation to you – find another one that will.

ANY OTHER QUESTIONS?

If you have *any* further 'What about...?' or 'What if...?' (or even 'Where exactly did you get that statistic on...?') questions – GREAT!

Ask a trusted financial or property advisor – or call the Custodian WealthBuilders Group in your state. My colleagues are all fellow wealth builders, and can help you answer (or ask) any questions you may have. Sceptics make the best wealth builders: we're comfortable with questions. (And answers.)

Contact details follow at the end of the book.

And finally...

Round-up quiz

As promised at the start of the book, here's an opportunity to demonstrate just how much you've learned and remembered of what you've read – and how good you are at looking for answers, once you know what the questions are.

I encourage you to have a go at this quiz now. Let yourself notice how easily the information sorts itself out, and how easily some of the answers come. (You may have to look up one or two: there's an index at the end of the book, if you need help.)

1. In making a wealth building investment decision, what would be more important?
   - ☐ How you felt about it
   - ☐ How it stacked up logically

2. What has shown the higher investment return over the last 10 years?
   - ☐ Shares
   - ☐ Residential property

3. In buying a residential investment property for wealth building, what would be more important?
   - ☐ Rental returns
   - ☐ Taxation benefits
   - ☐ Capital growth

4. If you invested in residential property, would you use the same criteria and decision-making process that you used to acquire your own home?
   - ☐ Yes
   - ☐ No

5. Is it prudent for me to acquire property close to where I live?

☐ Yes ☐ No

6. What would be more important in acquiring an investment property for wealth building?

☐ Managing your cash flow
☐ Buying the right property

7. What type of property would show the highest capital growth?

☐ Unit/townhouse
☐ House
☐ Land

8. If you had $50,000 deposit to invest in property, would you be better off buying:

☐ One property for $100,000?
☐ One property for $300,000?
☐ Two properties for $150,000 each?

9. The median house price in Brisbane rose from $30,500 in 1977 to $440,000 in 2009.

☐ True ☐ False

10. If you bought a house in 1967 in Melbourne, Sydney or Brisbane, by how much has its value increased in 2005?

☐ Doubled in value ☐ 10 times (1,000%)
☐ 5 times (500%) ☐ 20 times (2,000%)

11. Which institution(s) effectively control the affordability of housing in Australia?

    ☐ Real Estate Institute   ☐ Banks

    ☐ Property Developers   ☐ Valuers

12. Is the number of renters of property in Australia:

    ☐ Increasing?   ☐ Decreasing?

13. The Pay As You Go (PAYG) Income Tax (including Medicare levy) on a salary of $60,000 is approximately $12,150.

    ☐ True   ☐ False

14. Can I use my PAYG Tax to build wealth?

    ☐ Yes   ☐ No

15. In choosing a location that is going to give capital growth, which factor is most important?

    ☐ Proximity to transport

    ☐ Proximity to schools

    ☐ Percentage of investor-owners

    ☐ Established capital benchmark

16. You are seeking a bank loan for an investment property. Rank the following criteria in order of priority.

    ☐ Interest rate of loan

    ☐ Interest-only loan

    ☐ Full disclosure of bank valuation of investment property

    ☐ Non-collateralisation of other property

17. What is the 'established capital benchmark' of an area?
    - [ ] The median price of property in the area
    - [ ] The highest price of property in the area
    - [ ] The lowest price of property in the area

18. What was the average land size of an urban house in the capital cities in 1970?
    - [ ] 450m²
    - [ ] 600m²
    - [ ] 750m²
    - [ ] 1,000m²

19. What was the average land size of an urban house in the capital cities in 2005?
    - [ ] 450m²
    - [ ] 600m²
    - [ ] 750m²
    - [ ] 1,000m²

20. What was the percentage growth in the median price of a high-rise unit between 1990 and 2000?
    - [ ] 4%
    - [ ] 8%
    - [ ] 6%
    - [ ] 10%

Quiz answers

Now check our answers against yours – both in the Start-up Quiz on page 21 and in the Round-up Quiz you've just completed. Give yourself a score out of 14 for each quiz.

1. In making a wealth building investment decision, what would be more important?

    ☐ How you felt about it

    ☑ How it stacked up logically

2. What has shown the higher investment return over the last 10 years?

    ☐ Shares

    ☑ Residential property

3. In buying a residential investment property for wealth building, what would be more important?

    ☐ Rental returns

    ☐ Taxation benefits

    ☑ Capital growth

4. If you invested in residential property, would you use the same criteria and decision-making process that you used to acquire your own home?

    ☐ Yes   ☑ No

5. Is it prudent for me to acquire property close to where I live?

    ☐ Yes ☑ No

6. What would be more important in acquiring an investment property for wealth building?

    ☑ Managing your cash flow
    ☐ Buying the right property

7. What type of property would show the highest capital growth?

    ☐ Unit/townhouse
    ☐ House
    ☑ Land

8. If you had $50,000 deposit to invest in property, would you be better off buying:

    ☐ One property for $100,000?
    ☐ One property for $300,000?
    ☑ Two properties for $150,000 each?

9. The median house price in Brisbane rose from $30,500 in 1977 to $440,000 in 2009.

    ☑ True ☐ False

10. If you bought a house in 1967 in Melbourne, Sydney or Brisbane, by how much has its value increased in 2005?

　☐　Doubled in value　　☐　10 times (1,000%)
　☐　5 times (500%)　　　☑　20 times (2,000%)

11. Which institution(s) effectively control the affordability of housing in Australia?

　☐　Real Estate Institute
　☐　Property Developers
　☑　Banks
　☐　Valuers

12. Is the number of renters of property in Australia:

　☑　Increasing?
　☐　Decreasing?

13. The Pay As You Go (PAYG) Income Tax (including Medicare levy) on a salary of $60,000 is approximately $12,150.

　☑　True　　　　☐　False

14. Can I use my PAYG Tax to build wealth?

　☑　Yes　　　　☐　No

15. In choosing a location that is going to give capital growth, which factor is most important?

　☐　Proximity to transport
　☐　Proximity to schools
　☐　Percentage of investor-owners
　☑　Established capital benchmark

16. You are seeking a bank loan for an investment property. Rank the following criteria in order of priority.

    [4] Interest rate of loan

    [2] Interest only loan

    [1] Full disclosure of bank valuation of investment property

    [3] Non-collateralisation of other property

17. What is the 'established capital benchmark' of an area?

    ☐ The median price of property in the area

    ☑ The highest price of property in the area

    ☐ The lowest price of property in the area

18. What was the average land size of an urban house in the capital cities in 1970?

    ☐ 450m²   ☐ 600m²

    ☐ 750m²   ☑ 1,000m²

19. What was the average land size of an urban house in the capital cities in 2005?

    ☑ 450m²   ☐ 600m²

    ☐ 750m²   ☐ 1,000m²

20. What was the percentage growth in the median price of a high-rise unit between 1990 and 2000?

    ☑ 4%   ☐ 8%

    ☐ 6%   ☐ 10%

AND...

Pat yourself on the back. Seriously. Allow yourself to feel good about the knowledge and awareness you've developed. If you got some 'wrong' answers: great! That's often the best way to learn.

Especially if the whole property investment 'thing' was new to you, you may have had to take on board a load of unfamiliar terms and information and ideas. So you *know you can*. In fact, I hope you'll be reasonably confident that *you can build wealth*. You can do more – and be more – than perhaps you thought when you started this book.

If you've stayed with me for the whole eleven chapters: thanks. It gives me genuine satisfaction to have shared some of my experience and perspective with you – and to wonder what you might *do* with that information, and those ideas, and your own potential. (Feel free to drop me a line and let me know how you're going. I'd love to know – and will reply.) I hope you will become a fellow wealth builder and Custodian. But wherever you go from here:

may you be all you can be.

Standing poised in anticipation of challenge
and opportunities,
mind and body in balance,
He summons his talents to realise the
sanctioned visualisation.
With determination, integrity and conviction of truth,
service to humanity is his foundation.
He is honour bound.
"The Custodian"

The Custodian WealthBuilders Group

John Fitzgerald has developed a service to assist people to take the next step into wealth creation. John manages a property investment group called The Custodian WealthBuilders Group.

Services offered by the Custodian WealthBuilders Group include:
- Research and market analysis
- Finance
- Wealth building programs and workshops
- Property acquisition
- Property management

Contacts:

Head Office
JLF Corporation Head Office
Custodian House
7027 Southport-Nerang Road
Nerang QLD 4211 Australia
Phone: (07) 5527 4999
Free call: 1800 174 999
Fax: (07) 5527 4955
Email: info@jlf.com.au

Brisbane
Custodian WealthBuilders
172 Robertson Street
Fortitude Valley QLD 4006
Phone: (07) 3831 4135
Fax: (07) 3831 4262
Email: info@custodian.com.au

New South Wales
Custodian WealthBuilders
Suite 302, Level 3
213-219 Miller Street
North Sydney NSW 2060
Phone: (02) 8904 0555
Fax: (02) 8904 0499
Email: info@wealthbuilders.com.au

Australian Capital Territory
Custodian WealthBuilders
Street U14-14, Brierly Street
Postal PO Box 3715
Weston ACT 2611
Phone: (02) 6287 2880
Email: canberra@custodian.com.au

Victoria
Level 2/100 Dorcas Street
Building E, Kings Garden
South Melbourne, VIC 3205
Phone: (03) 9699 4955
Fax: (03) 9699 6233
Email: info@custwb.com.au

Western Australia
Suite 3, Level 1
45 Royal Street
East Perth WA 6004
Free call: 1800 801 553
Fax: (08) 9221 8002
Email: perth@custodian.com.au

Websites: www.wealthbuilders.com.au
www.jlf.com.au
www.toogoolawa.com.au
www.untoldwealth.com.au
www.signpoststosuccess.com.au
www.signpoststosuccess.co.uk

Custodian Helpline: 1800 174 999

If you have any comments on this book, or would like to let us know how the wealth building concept is working for you, you are most welcome to write to John Fitzgerald at the head office.

If you would like further copies of *Seven Steps to Wealth*, or *We Can Be Heroes*, please contact the Custodian office nearest you, or post or fax one of the order forms provided at the back of this copy.

If you would to attend one of John Fitzgerald's Custodian WealthBuilders workshops, or require further information on any of our services, please telephone 1800 174 999.

Investloan

Finance brokers who specialise in residential investment property loans. Accreditation with the Australian Finance Group gives us access to over 30 lenders Australia-wide.

Queensland
172 Robertson Street
Fortitude Valley QLD 4006
Phone: (07) 3831 3022
Fax: (07) 3831 4262
Email: info@investloan.com.au

New South Wales
Suite 302, 213-219 Miller Street
North Sydney NSW 2060
Phone: (02) 8904 1322
Fax: (02) 8904 1328
Email: sydney@investloan.com.au

Victoria
Level 2/100 Dorcas Street
Building E, Kings Garden
South Melbourne, VIC 3205
Phone: (03) 9699 4955
Fax: (03) 9699 6233
Email: melblenders@investloan.com.au

Western Australia
Suite 3, First Floor, 45 Royal Street
East Perth WA 6004
Phone: (08) 9221 7004
Fax: (08) 9221 8002
Email: perth@investloan.com

The Toogoolawa Children's Home Ltd

Contacts:

Drs Ron & Suwanti Farmer

Toogoolawa Children's Home Ltd & Toogoolawa Schools Project

39 Gerrale Drive, Willow Vale, QLD 4209

Telephone: (07) 5546 7998 or (07) 5596 6866

Facsimile: (07) 5546 6099

suronfar@technet2000.com.au

Book Order form

Seven Steps to wealth...

To: Toogoolawa Schools Ltd,
PO Box 2256, Nerang MDC, Qld 4211
Fax: (07) 5527 4955

CONTACT DETAILS (All personal information is kept confidential)

Name: _____

Address: _____

_____ Postcode: _____

(AH): _____ (W): _____ (Mob): _____

Email: _____

Please send me the following copies:

1) 'We Can Be Heroes' by John L Fitzgerald:

   Quantity _____ @ $19.95 each   Subtotal: $_____
   (inclusive of GST)

2) 'Seven Steps to Wealth' by John L Fitzgerald:

   Quantity _____ @ $21.95 each   Subtotal: $_____
   (inclusive of GST)

3) 'Love Changes Everything' by Dr Ron Farmer:

   Quantity _____ @ $21.95 each   Subtotal: $_____
   (inclusive of GST)

Plus postage & packaging @ $5.00 per book Subtotal: $_____

I would like to make a general donation to Toogoolawa of $_____

(Bulk rates available on request)   Total: $_____

PAYMENT DETAILS

☐ I enclose a cheque/money order made payable to The Toogoolawa Schools Ltd.

☐ Please debit my credit card.

No: _ _ _ _ / _ _ _ _ / _ _ _ _ / _ _ _ _   Expiry Date: _ _ / _ _

Type: ☐ Visa ☐ Mastercard ☐ American Express

Name as it appears on card (please print):

_____

Authorisation signature: _____
Please allow 28 days for delivery

Donation form

Please register my donation with the Toogoolawa Schools Ltd with one of the following:

☐ Regular donation of $_____ via Direct Debit

I will be donating ☐ Weekly ☐ Fortnightly ☐ Monthly
(Please send me bank details)

☐ I would like to make a general donation of $_____
(I have filled in payment details below)

☐ Please send me information on how I, or anyone in my workplace, can contribute using the Workplace Giving program.

CONTACT DETAILS (All personal information is kept confidential)

Name: _____
Address: _____
_____ Postcode: _____
(AH): _____ (W): _____ (Mob): _____
Email: _____

PAYMENT DETAILS

☐ I enclose a cheque/money order made payable to The Toogoolawa Schools Ltd.

☐ Please debit my credit card.

No: _ _ _ _ / _ _ _ _ / _ _ _ _ / _ _ _ _   Expiry Date: _ _ / _ _

Type: ☐ Visa ☐ Mastercard ☐ American Express

Name as it appears on card (please print):
_____

Authorisation signature: _____

Please send me a tax receipt ☐ per donation ☐ per financial year
(All contributions over $2 are tax deductible)

Ready for the next step...?

Untold Wealth: Success from Scratch

Books and seminars – by themselves – don't build wealth. You have to get out there and do it. And unfortunately, it's the starting that stops most people. It can seem like a big first step.

That's why John Fitzgerald developed *Untold Wealth: Success from Scratch*. It's a comprehensive tool kit for building wealth through property. Starting wherever you are. No start-up knowledge? No start-up capital? No worries. This is Success from Scratch.

A complete system for **passive wealth building,** based on the proven principles of *Seven Steps to Wealth*. A powerful system for **active wealth building** – if (or when) you're ready to go there. Ambitious goal-setting; creative financing, negotiating and networking; identifying undervalued assets – and realising their potential.

THE PROGRAM INCLUDES:

Start-up DVD: a brief *'face to face'* welcome from John Fitzgerald.

A comprehensive 300-page **workbook,** with all the knowledge, skills and tools you need to get started – and to *move on*.

The best selling book ***Seven Steps to Wealth:*** a solid foundation in wealth building concepts and techniques.

Three CD set: *Success, Focus and Accelerated Wealth*. Designed to support your learning – and your motivation – to set and meet challenging financial goals.

We Can Be Heroes: the stories of extraordinary Australians who have invested more than money – and found purpose and passion in return.

Goal Workbook: a fantastic annual tool that will keep you motivated

'It's something that I urge you to investigate because it's not only educational; it's just the greatest fun. I set a goal on 10 properties and I achieved that last year.'
Margaret Seedsman

If you do not feel that *Untold Wealth: Success From Scratch* is the most powerful wealth building program you have ever experienced, simply return it within 30 days for a full refund of the purchase price (excluding p&h). You can even keep the Australian best seller *Seven Steps to Wealth* and the inspirational and uplifting book *We Can Be Heroes* as our special gift to you.

$299.00 or
$149.50 x 2 months (for credit card holders only)
Plus $19.99 p&h

Call 1800 554 622
www.untoldwealth.com.au
Operators available 24 hours 7 days a week

Signposts to Success

Signposts to Success is designed to sharpen your sense of direction. To get you past wishing and into focused action. To get you through barriers: the ones the world throws at you – and the ones you build yourself. To set you up for success – whatever that means for you.

Signposts to Success doesn't focus on any particular investment vehicle or business model. Its focus is on personal and interpersonal skills and strategies that underpin any successful performance. Maybe you're looking to start an investment program, or your own business.

Maybe you're already in the thick of it – and struggling to keep your head above water. Maybe you're not doing anything right now... *Signposts to Success* may be for you.

THE PROGRAM INCLUDES:

A comprehensive 274-page **workbook,** talking about where you want to get to – and how you can get there.

Includes:

Three CD set: *Signposts, Success and Focus.* Designed to support your learning – and your motivation – to set and meet challenging success goals.

We Can Be Heroes: the stories of extraordinary Australians who have invested more than money – and found purpose and passion in return.

If you do not feel that *Signposts to Success* is the most powerful success program you have ever experienced, simply return it within 30 days for a full refund of the purchase price (excluding p&h).

You can even keep the inspirational and uplifting book *We Can Be Heroes* as our special gift to you.

$150.00 or
$50.00 x 3 months (for credit card holders only)
Plus $19.95 p&h

Call 1800 888 805
www.signpoststosuccess.com.au
Operators available 24 hours 7 days a week

201

Index

A
achieve your potential, 62
affordability, 62, 129–133, 144
 history, 152
 market, 134
'all monies' clauses, 115, 121
assets, acquisition of, 32
average total weekly earnings, 131

B
bank valuations, 5, 113–116, 120, 176
banks
 insurance indemnity, 116
 lending, 5–6, 37
 margin call, 40, 41
 second-tier, 121
Bigger Fool Theory, 12–13
book-keeping as tax deduction, 108
brokers, 122–3
buildings
 depreciation, 65
 replacement cost, 112
 tax deductions, 104
buyer beware, 5
bank valuations, 113–115
 comparable investment sales, 6–7
 statistics, 6

C
Capital Gains Tax (CGT), 147–149
capital growth potential, 3–4, 32
 of land, 4, 13, 14–15, 60, 65, 68, 72
capital thinking, 27
capital vs. income, 29–30, 32
cash flow management, 32, 56, 105, 124
Cockerel, Bert, 11
commercial sector, 40–43

commission, vendor pays, 5
comparable sales, 113, 117
compound growth, 3, 32, 38, 58–59
counter-cyclical buying, 142
Cousins Real Estate, 12
cross-collateralisation, 115, 119
Custodian WealthBuilders, 17, 30, 31

D
Dainford Limited, 13, 14–15, 71
debt levels, 28–29
depreciation, 104–106
 buildings, 65
 new versus old houses, 110
 properties built since 1985, 104
dual occupancy, 150
duplexes, land value, 67

E
economic cycles, 127
equity, 39
 definition, 37, 38
 growth of, 57
 protecting, 115, 119
established capital benchmark, 76–77

F
Farmer, Ron, 16, 157, 164
Farmer, Suwanti, 16, 157
finance to build, 62
financial goal, 139
fittings. see fixtures and fittings
Fitzgerald, John
 background, 7–8
 start of real estate career, 11–12
fixtures and fittings
 depreciation, 105, 106

Index | 203

G
gearing, 29, 37, 56, 101
Get Rich Quick thinking, 1
Global Financial Crisis (GFC), 38, 41, 42, 43, 80, 129, 132, 133, 152
Goods and Services Tax (GST), 149, 169–170
goodwill, 40–41
'grocery' money, 108
growth, structure for, 32, 51, 53–54, 60

H
high density zoning, 150
house prices 1991, 142
houses
    constructed before 1985, 108–109
    land value, 67
    national median house price, 131
    new versus old, 109, 110
    replacement cost, 112–113
housing affordability. see affordability

I
income
    optimisation of, 62, 81–95
    vs. capital, 29–30
income thinking, 27
insurance
    bank indemnity, 116
    landlord protection, 93–94
    mortgage, 120
    against unemployment, 171
interest only loans, 124
interest rate negotiation, 122
interest rates, 170
    locking in, 124–125
interstate travel, 108
Investloan, 123
investment
    accessing value, 111–113, 117
    in Australia, 108, 125
    bank valuations, 5, 113–116, 120
    multiple, 125
    in older properties, 108–9
    pace of growth, 137–141
    returns 1985-2009, 36
    step by step, 144–145

J
JLF Corporation, 15

L
land
    capital growth potential, 4, 13, 14–15, 60, 65, 72–80
    estates, 14–15
location of, 72–73
land tax, 70–71
land value, 4–5, 65–67, 68–72, 112
landlord protection insurance, 93–94
leverage, 37, 38–39
loan providers
    brokers, 122–3
    choosing, 118–125
    guidelines, 121
    interest rate negotiation, 122
loan value ratio (LVR), 115, 118, 119
loans
    affordability, 120, 129
    conversion to P & I, 145–146
    fees, 120
    interest only, 124
    interest rate, lock in, 124–125
    problems, 171
    repaying by selling, 146–149
    separate, 115

M
Margolis, George, 11–12
marketing fees, vendor pays, 5

median house price, 131
mortgage insurance, 120
mortgage repayments, 129–130

N
negative gearing, 101–102, 106–110
   abolition, 173–174
net worth. see equity
1982 crash, 13

O
office buildings, 42–43
outlays, 109

P
PAYG Income Tax Withholding Variation (ITWV) Application, 107
pension, 28
principal & interest (P&I) loans, 145–146
property
   assessing value, 5, 113–116, 120
   average growth, 142
   average prices, 131
   bank valuations, 5, 6, 113–116
   buying reasons, 3
   high density zoning, 150
   lower-end, value, 133, 134–145
   monitoring value, 131
   multiple investments, 125
   outlays, 109
   pre 1985, investment value, 108–109
   security value, 120
   selling to repay debt, 146–149
   separate loans, 115
   top end, value, 133
property boom (2003-08), 129
property cycle. see real estate cycle

Q
quantity surveyor's report, 106
quiz, 21–24, 181–184

R
rates notices, 112
real estate. see also property
   basic questions, 5
   building a portfolio, 58–59, 111, 137–141
   losing money, 1–2
   managing a portfolio, 175–176
   on-selling, 12
real estate cycle, 127–128, 134, 142–3, 146
real estate industry
   buyer beware, 5
   size, 1
regional areas, 78–79
rental income
   market rate, 88–90, 91
   optimisation, 83–85, 88–90
rental property
   cover unexpected costs, 93–94
   demand for, 82–83
   insurance, 93–94
   managing agents, 95
   tax deductions, 102–103, 108
   tenant issues, 172–173
   tenants, screening, 92–93
   vacancy factor, 86–88
residential sector, 43. *see also* houses
   choosing a home, 45–46
   choosing an investment property, 46–47
   choosing for capital growth, 47–48, 65–67
   demand, factors affecting, 74–76, 80, 85–86

land content, 67
leverage, 37–38
market history, 152
performance, 36–37
security, 34–35
size, 1
tax deductions, 104
wealth, source of, 32
retirement income, 25–26
return on investment 1985-2009, 36

S
security value of property, 120
selling property, 146–149
shares, 38
shopping centres, 42

T
Tax Administration Act 1953, 107, 108
tax benefits, maximisation, 62
tax deductions
    book-keeping, 108
    interest only loans, 124
    interstate travel, 108
    non-cash deductible items, 104–106
    rental property, 102–103
taxes, 147–149, 169–170
tenancy application form, 96–99
time, making it work for you, 62
Toogoolawa Children's Home, 157–158
Toogoolawa project, 161–164
Toogoolawa Schools, 158–160
townhouses, land value, 4, 67
travel as tax deductions, 108
true capital worth. see equity

U
unemployment, 171–172
unimproved land values, 112

units
    investment, 6–7, 12–13, 68–72
    land value, 4–5, 67, 68–72
urban infill, 150

V
vacancy factor, 86–88
Valuer General's Office, 112, 113, 116
valuers, 116–117
    banks, 5, 113–116, 120, 176

W
wealth building
    custodian role, 16–17, 31, 155–157, 164–165
    definition, 32
    services, what to look for, 30
    seven basic steps, 60
    starting point, 57–58

Z
zero-cost financing, 114, 123